Toxic Shock Syndrome

Titles in the Diseases and Disorders series include:

DISEASES & DISORDERS

Toxic Shock Syndrome

Barbara Sheen

LUCENT BOOKS

An imprint of Thomson Gale, a part of The Thomson Corporation

THOMSON
™
GALE

Detroit • New York • San Francisco • San Diego • New Haven, Conn.
Waterville, Maine • London • Munich

THOMSON

ᵀᴹ

GALE

On Cover: The purple bodies in this color-enhanced electron micrograph are *Staphylococcus aureus* bacteria, which are a factor in causing some people to develop toxic shock syndrome.

LIBRARY OF CONGRESS CATALOGING-IN-PUBLICATION DATA

Sheen, Barbara.
    Toxic shock syndrome / by Barbara Sheen.
        p. cm. — (Diseases and disorders series)
    Includes bibliographical references and index.
    Contents: A mysterious illness—Overactivating the immune system—A medical emergency—Recovery and prevention—Protecting the public now and in the future.
    ISBN 1-59018-859-4 (hardcover : alk. paper) 1. Toxic shock syndrome—Juvenile literature. I. Title. II. Series.
RG220.S44 2006
616.9'297—dc22
                                                                                2005032620

Printed in China

Table of Contents

"The Most Difficult Puzzles Ever Devised"

Charles Best, one of the pioneers in the search for a cure for diabetes, once explained what it is about medical research that intrigued him so. "It's not just the gratification of knowing one is helping people," he confided, "although that probably is a more heroic and selfless motivation. Those feelings may enter in, but truly, what I find best is the feeling of going toe to toe with nature, of trying to solve the most difficult puzzles ever devised. The answers are there somewhere, those keys that will solve the puzzle and make the patient well. But how will those keys be found?"

Since the dawn of civilization, nothing has so puzzled people— and often frightened them, as well—as the onset of illness in a body or mind that had seemed healthy before. A seizure, the inability of a heart to pump, the sudden deterioration of muscle tone in a small child—being unable to reverse such conditions or even to understand why they occur was unspeakably frustrating to healers. Even before there were names for such conditions, even before they were understood at all, each was a reminder of how complex the human body was, and how vulnerable.

While our grappling with understanding diseases has been frustrating at times, it has also provided some of humankind's most heroic accomplishments. Alexander Fleming's accidental discovery in 1928 of a mold that could be turned into penicillin has resulted in the saving of untold millions of lives. The isolation of the enzyme insulin has reversed what was once a death sentence for anyone with diabetes. There have been great strides in combating conditions for which there is not yet a cure, too. Medicines can help AIDS patients live longer, diagnostic tools such as mammography and ultrasounds can help doctors find tumors while they are treatable, and laser surgery techniques have made the most intricate, minute operations routine.

This "toe-to-toe" competition with diseases and disorders is even more remarkable when seen in a historical continuum. An astonishing amount of progress has been made in a very short time. Just two hundred years ago, the existence of germs as a cause of some diseases was unknown. In fact, it was less than 150 years ago that a British surgeon named Joseph Lister had difficulty persuading his fellow doctors that washing their hands before delivering a baby might increase the chances of a healthy delivery (especially if they had just attended to a diseased patient)!

Each book in Lucent's Diseases and Disorders series explores a disease or disorder and the knowledge that has been accumulated (or discarded) by doctors through the years. Each book also examines the tools used for pinpointing a diagnosis, as well as the various means that are used to treat or cure a disease. Finally, new ideas are presented—techniques or medicines that may be on the horizon.

Frustration and disappointment are still part of medicine, for not every disease or condition can be cured or prevented. But the limitations of knowledge are being pushed outward constantly; the "most difficult puzzles ever devised" are finding challengers every day.

Knowledge Is Crucial

Leslie was a healthy young mother when she suddenly developed what she thought was a very bad case of the flu. Her condition did not improve with bed rest, however; instead, her health rapidly deteriorated. By the time she sought medical care, her blood pressure had dropped dangerously low, she was going into shock, and her organs were beginning to fail. She was immediately admitted to the hospital, where her condition was deemed so grave that her family was warned she might not survive. "I could tell by the way everybody was hovering over me, a couple of times they thought they were going to lose me. . . . I was really scared,"[1] she explains.

Later, Leslie learned that she had had toxic shock syndrome (TSS), a rare bacterial illness that can cause death in a matter of hours. Like many but not all female victims, Leslie was menstruating when the illness struck. And her symptoms mirrored those that most characterize TSS. But the condition garners little attention from the media, and Leslie was not aware of the danger signs. As a result, she did not seek medical help until it was almost too late.

A Rare and Potentially Fatal Illness

Whereas heart disease strikes 1 million Americans annually and breast cancer strikes two hundred thousand, only one hundred to three hundred contract TSS. Between six and eighteen TSS victims die each year, usually within a week of becoming sick. Yet in many instances TSS can be prevented, and if the ill-

8

ness does strike, its severity can be modulated by seeking medical attention when symptoms first appear. "While TSS is rare, it is an important health concern," U.S. Food and Drug Administration (FDA) staff writer Dixie Farley writes. "Knowing how to prevent it and recognizing its symptoms can do much to reduce its dangers and continue to keep its incidence low."[2]

Lack of Knowledge

Unfortunately, most individuals do not know enough about TSS to protect themselves or their loved ones. Since the likelihood

A man comforts his wife in the hospital. Prompt medical attention can prevent toxic shock syndrome from becoming life threatening.

of developing TSS is slim, most people are not concerned about contracting the condition. Therefore, they do not think it is necessary to learn about TSS. "Nobody gets those rare diseases. . . . It doesn't happen to real people," Leslie says. "A disease, especially if it's weird and unusual is something that happens to someone else. [But] sometimes," she adds, "you are the someone else."[3]

Adding to the problem, misconceptions about TSS abound, and many individuals think that the illness was eliminated more than two decades ago. Tracy, whose sixteen-year-old daughter, Kourtney, died of TSS in 2005, thought the syndrome was a thing of the past until Kourtney contracted the illness. She explains: "Since they hadn't been talking about this in years you think you are safe. . . . My daughter is gone. . . . I'm

It is important that older family members explain the risk of toxic shock syndrome to young girls.

never going to see her get married. I'm never going to see her have kids. . . . And to be struck down by this? That's hard."[4]

The Importance of Awareness

Although there is no way to ensure that what happened to Kourtney will not happen to anyone else, learning about TSS can reduce that risk. Awareness of what causes the condition, what measures people can take to decrease the chance of the illness developing, and what signs and symptoms to look for can save lives.

Older family members can help educate the young. Since menstruation and tampon use has been linked to TSS, providing youthful female family members with information about TSS is important. Bea, whose cousin lost her life to TSS, explains:

> My cousin died of toxic shock syndrome. It was due to her using tampons. She got sick, but thought it was a virus and didn't go to the doctor for days. All the while, she kept using tampons, which is probably the worst thing a person with TSS can do. It just made her sicker. But she didn't know that and neither did any of the family. If we had known more, maybe she wouldn't have died. But none of us had even heard of toxic shock syndrome before she died. Her death changed that. My nieces are too young to remember their cousin or what happened to her. They don't know anything about TSS. But they should. As soon as each of my girls started menstruating, I talked to them about toxic shock. I don't want to scare them, but they need to know how to protect themselves. Yes, toxic shock is rare but people still get it, it's still around. Young girls need to know how to use tampons wisely. And, they need to know what to do if they start feeling sick and not do the wrong thing or wait until it is too late, like their cousin did.[5]

When it comes to TSS, knowledge is crucial. In fact, learning about the condition can save a person's life.

CHAPTER ONE

A Mysterious Illness

Toxic shock syndrome is a rare, potentially life-threatening illness characterized by fever, low blood pressure, shock, and circulatory system failure. It is defined by the U.S. Centers for Disease Control and Prevention (CDC) as: "An acute syndrome involving high fever, a scarlet fever–like rash, skin peeling, radically lower blood pressure, and at least 3 of the following systematic symptoms: diarrhea, vomiting, muscle aches, vaginal or throat infections, kidney malfunction, liver failure, disorientation or confusion."[6]

The condition develops when small colonies of the bacteria *Staphylococcus aureus* (*S. aureus*) overgrow and secrete toxins into an affected individual's bloodstream. The illness is often related to menstruation, a staphylococcus infection due to surgery, a burn, or an open sore. Although TSS can strike both males and females, more than 90 percent of all cases involve women of childbearing age.

The condition was relatively unknown until late 1979, when, in an eight-month period, fifty-five healthy women were stricken with a mysterious illness that rapidly worsened, causing alarming drops in blood pressure followed by shock. Seven of the women died.

The unknown illness mystified medical professionals. But by analyzing each case and establishing links between them, experts were able to unravel some of the mysteries surrounding the illness, thereby saving lives.

Three Boys and Four Girls

Although most medical professionals were unfamiliar with the puzzling sickness, while unnamed, it was not a new condition. A few cases with similar characteristics were described as far back as 1927. These involved military personnel with battle or surgical wounds. Nevertheless, such cases occurred so infrequently that most medical experts had little or no knowledge of the condition.

Then, in the three-year period beginning in 1975, Dr. James K. Todd of the Children's Hospital in Denver reported seven

A high fever is a common symptom of toxic shock syndrome.

cases. These affected three males and four females between the ages of eight and seventeen.

These cases baffled Todd. He could not explain what had caused these otherwise healthy young people suddenly to become seriously ill. He noted that each of the males had an open sore, no matter how minor, somewhere on their bodies. The first case, for instance, was a sixteen-year-old boy. Todd recalls, "The youngster's only source of illness was a small abscess [a pus-filled sore] on his buttock."[7]

The females, on the other hand, had no visible sores. Two of the four had a mild inflammation of the vagina, a condition known as vaginitis. All were menstruating at the time, and three of the four girls were using tampons.

Todd theorized that an unknown pathogen had somehow gained entry into the patients' bloodstreams, causing systematic damage to their bodies. Cell cultures and blood samples indicated the presence of *Staphylococcus aureus* not in the patients' blood, but in fluid-bathed areas such as the throat, the nose, the vagina, or a sore. Consequently, Todd reasoned that the bacteria secreted toxins, proteins that act like poisons, into the victims' blood.

He speculated that the bacteria had entered the male patients through the open sores. The females with vaginitis, which often causes the vaginal walls to dry out and peel, might have acquired microscopic cuts in the vaginal walls through which the bacteria gained entry. Vaginitis also can weaken the immune system, increasing a patient's susceptibility to infection. But the doctor could not explain how the unknown toxin gained entry into the bloodstreams of two female patients without vaginitis or why they had become sick.

Naming the Illness

Todd carefully searched the medical literature but could not find a previously named illness that matched his patients' symptoms. Based on the fact that the bacteria produced toxins that, if uncontrolled, caused shock, Todd named the illness

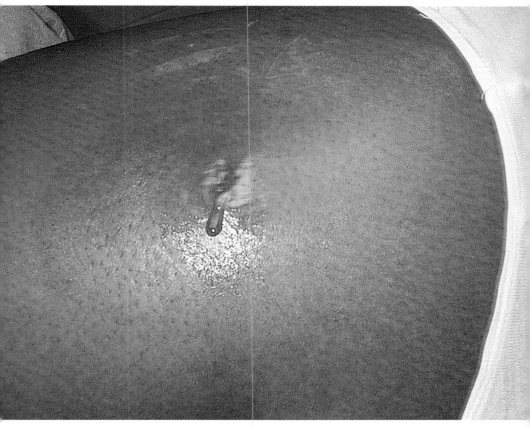

This abscess was the result of *Staphylococcus aureus* bacteria, which also causes toxic shock syndrome.

toxic shock syndrome. In medical language, a syndrome is an illness with regular symptoms and no known cause.

In 1978, Todd described the seven cases in a report published in the *Lancet*, a medical journal, but did not define the condition. The article and the new condition it named received little attention by the medical community.

More Cases, Mainly Women

Then, between October 1979 and May 1980, fifty-five similar cases with a 13 percent fatality rate developed. Unlike Todd's juvenile patients, 95 percent of the patients were women of childbearing age. But like the two cases that perplexed Todd, none had any sores or infections.

This was an unprecedented number of cases occurring in a much shorter time frame than had previously been recorded. To put this in perspective, three cases were reported in one four-day period in Wisconsin alone, compared to the seven cases that Todd treated, which occurred over a three-year period.

Because Todd's report received little notice and dealt primarily with children, the possibility that the patients were suffering from TSS was not considered. In fact, most of the attending physicians had never heard of the condition and were, therefore, unaware of the threat it posed. Consequently, most of these early cases were labeled and treated as less serious illnesses or as an unnamed condition. By the time the affected individuals were admitted to the hospital, most were dangerously ill.

That was what happened to Pat Kehm in 1980. Author Tom Riley describes what occurred when Pat's husband, Mike, took her to the emergency room for the first time:

> The emergency room doctor observed that Pat's throat was inflamed. Suspecting strep throat . . . he gave her some anti-vomiting pills and a shot of penicillin—an antibiotic that is effective against many bacteria but not *Staphylococcus aureus*. . . . Unaware of the cause of Pat Kehm's clinical symptoms, the emergency room physician sent her home with the suggestion she see her doctor on Monday if she didn't "perk up." On the way home from the emergency room the first circumstantial sign of shock appeared. Pat was dizzy when Mike took her back to the car, an indication that her brain cells were being deprived of the normal amount of oxygen.[8]

The next day Pat Kehm did go see her doctor. At that point, her blood pressure was so low that it could not be measured by standard means, and her heart and lungs were failing. She was admitted to the hospital immediately. Efforts to save Kehm failed. Her death certificate listed the cause of her death as cardiac arrest. But her doctor later said it was TSS that caused her heart to cease functioning.

Making Connections

New cases continued to emerge. Although the condition remained unidentified, by December 31, 1980, state health departments reported a total of 1,392 cases to the CDC in Atlanta, whose job it is to prevent and control the spread of infectious diseases. The vast majority of these cases were in otherwise healthy women.

The high incidence of cases occurring in a brief time span alerted the CDC to the potentiality of an epidemic. Therefore, CDC epidemiologists, whose job it is to investigate the transmission and control of epidemic diseases, were alerted.

To avert an epidemic, it was necessary to identify the condition, determine its cause, and eliminate it. Therefore, epidemiologists analyzed and compared the symptoms described in the state reports to those of other cases contained in an extensive data bank maintained by the CDC. The symptoms matched those described by Todd, and the illness was identified as TSS. The CDC then constructed a definition for the disorder, which helped the investigators to distinguish between TSS and illnesses with similar symptoms. This enabled epidemiologists to track and study the illness better.

At the same time, the CDC classified TSS as an emergent disease—that is, a disease or syndrome that was once rare but has suddenly become more common and threatens to increase in the future. Emergent diseases pose a threat to society because lack of knowledge about their cause makes them hard to control. Therefore, the importance of finding and eliminating the cause of TSS intensified.

Digging Deeper

In an attempt to do this, the CDC once again examined the state reports, looking for similarities among the patients. The

Streptococcus Toxic Shock Syndrome

Toxic shock syndrome is caused by *Staphylococcus aureus.* A related illness is caused by another microbe. Streptococcus toxic shock syndrome, or STSS, most often occurs after streptococcus bacteria invade areas around a minor skin wound or chicken pox blister. It almost never follows a simple streptococcus throat infection like strep throat.

People with STSS exhibit similar symptoms to those with TSS: fever, weakness, difficulty breathing, a rash, and low blood pressure, which leads to shock. In some cases, the area around the skin wound or chicken pox blister swells, reddens, and dies. This means the flesh becomes gangrenous (dead). The life-threatening condition known as necrotizing fasciitis, often called the flesh eating disease, can result.

Necrotizing fasciitis occurs in STSS but not in TSS. Once the condition appears, it spreads rapidly throughout the body, causing severe pain as skin, muscle, and fat cells die. Dead tissue must be surgically removed to save the life of the patient. Often this means that affected body parts must be amputated.

data indicated that 95 percent of the patients were menstruating females, and the others had visible signs of infection such as abscesses and/or surgical or other wounds. This information, however, did not bring investigators any closer to the source of the illness.

In June 1980, the CDC surveyed fifty-two survivors of verified cases of TSS and fifty-two age- and gender-matched participants in a control group. The members of the control group, who never had TSS, were compared to the TSS survivors to validate the findings. Both groups were limited to women of childbearing age, since this group comprised the great majority of TSS victims.

STSS is more deadly than TSS. Approximately 50 percent of all patients with STSS die. And, although STSS is rare, it is more common than TSS, with an estimated ten to twenty cases occurring for every ten thousand people.

This scientist at the Centers for Disease Control and Prevention (CDC) is performing a test to identify bacteria. The CDC made the connection between tampon use and toxic shock syndrome.

The subjects answered questions about their general health, sexual activities, and menstrual cycles. Questions about the subjects' use of menstrual products such as tampons and sanitary pads were also posed. By comparing the responses of the TSS survivors to those of the control group, the investigators hoped to discover any differences between the two groups. Bruce Dan, an epidemiologist involved in the study, elaborates: "The CDC's main mission is to prevent unnecessary disease and death. The way we do that very quickly is to do a quick retrospective study looking at people who got the disease and people who did not, to find out what was the critical factor, and hopefully eliminate the critical factor."[9]

The results were interesting. As the investigators suspected, the onset of TSS occurred while all of the TSS survivors were menstruating. There were no significant differences between the two groups' general health, sexual activities, or menstrual cycles. Differences were apparent, however, in tampon usage. All of the TSS survivors had used tampons exclusively and had been using them at the time of their illness. In comparison, forty-four of the fifty-two subjects in the control group used tampons, but only ten of this group used the devices exclusively. The other thirty-four subjects alternated between tam-

Harvard scientist Edward H. Kass holds a beaker containing tampon fibers, which are believed to be a cause of toxic shock syndrome.

pons and sanitary pads. As a result, the investigators concluded that a link existed between prolonged tampon usage and the development of TSS. Author Tom Riley explains why the scientists reached this conclusion: "In the science of statistics, such a difference in tampon usage between case and control is deemed statistically significant—meaning that it is improbable that the association of tampons with TSS victims was a coincidence."[10]

Why Now?

Since tampons were not new but TSS was, the link to tampons did not solve the mystery. To learn why the outbreak was occurring, CDC scientists needed to determine what had changed between the periods of few and relatively many cases. Upon re-analyzing the survey data in terms of type of tampons used by both groups, scientists found significant statistical differences. Seventy-one percent of the TSS survivors had used a new type of super-absorbent tampon recently released on the market, as compared to 26 percent of the control group. The investigators theorized that the new product had somehow triggered the development of TSS in some users. However, they did not know why this was so.

The New Tampons

The scientists hoped that by determining how the new tampons differed from traditional ones, they could pinpoint the link between the devices and the development of TSS. The new tampons were promoted as having an innovative design and construction that allowed them to be worn all night without leakage. In contrast, traditional tampons need to be changed about every four hours.

Unlike traditional tampons, which are made of cotton and rayon, the super-absorbent type was composed of a highly absorbent mix of polyester foam and cellulose. This blend of synthetic foam and natural cellulose fibers soaks up fluids like a sponge. Indeed, according to a 1981 statement by the FDA, "the new tampons were capable of absorbing more

Medical Detectives

Epidemiologists are medical detectives who investigate diseases. These scientists travel throughout the world wherever an outbreak of a rare or unknown disease occurs. In an interview on the Web site Stalking the Mysterious Microbe, sponsored by the American Society of Microbiology, Centers for Disease Control and Prevention epidemiologist Ali S. Khan, MD, talks about his job.

"My job is probably no different from any other detective in the world, except I try to figure out how people in a community are getting sick. What we do is, we've got to find all the clues first. Then, we've got to put all those little clues together like a puzzle to try to figure out what's going on in the community—who was the first person sick, who was the second, who was the third, what were their associations, what were the things that they did that got them infected. And the nice thing about what we do as disease detectives is that we don't just solve a mystery. Once we solve it, that tells us how we can actually make a difference— how we can make this disease go away."

Stalking the Mysterious Microbe, "Ali S. Khan, Disease Detective." www.microbe. org/careers/Khan.asp.

fluid than most women actually had in their vagina at any given time."[11]

In addition, the two materials formed a weblike structure with small air pockets or chambers, which trapped moisture and stretched as the tampon became thick with fluid. Therefore, as menses fluid was absorbed, the surface area of the tampon increased and the tampon expanded like a teabag until it completely filled the vaginal cavity and touched the vaginal walls. Any menstrual fluids not absorbed were essentially dammed up as long as the tampon remained in place, and leakage was prevented.

The Problem with Super Absorbency

Although preventing menstrual leakage, the new tampon had some unintended consequences. It was these effects, the investigators theorized, that encouraged the development of TSS. Although the theory has never been proven conclusively, it is widely accepted by the scientific community. The theory is based on the fact that many women harbor small amounts of *S. aureus* in their vaginas. Conditions in the vagina, however, keep the bacteria from overgrowing and releasing toxins. The ability of the tampon to absorb and trap large quantities of

Using tampons (lower right)—particularly the super-absorbent variety—can foster the overgrowth of *Staphylococcus aureus*.

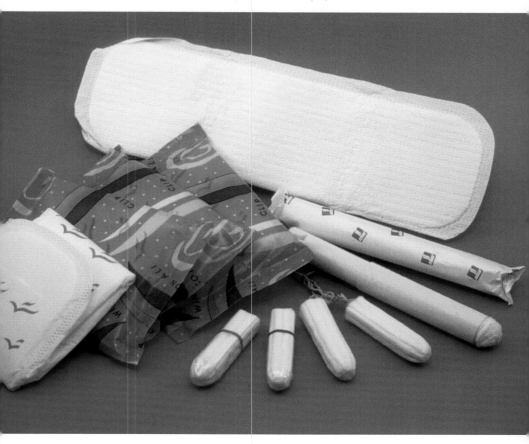

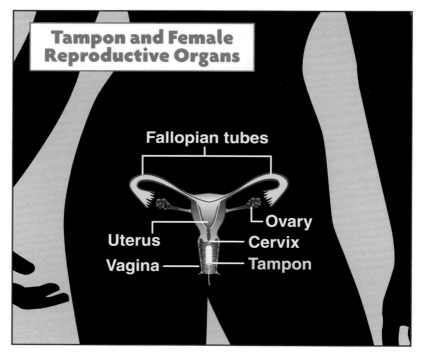

Tampon and Female Reproductive Organs

Fallopian tubes

Uterus

Vagina

Ovary

Cervix

Tampon

menstrual fluids in oxygen-rich pockets changed these conditions, creating an environment that triggered bacterial overgrowth and subsequent toxin production. Leaving the tampon in place for long periods exacerbated this process by keeping the bacteria and toxins close to the body, where they could do the most harm. New Mexico State University emeritus professor of chemistry Dr. Robert V. Hoffman explains:

> The tampon had a large surface, was highly porous, and had lots of air. *S. aureus* is an aerobic bacteria, which means it needs oxygen. The tampon provided the bacteria with air, a warm environment, a moist environment—a perfect foundation for growth. You had lots of proteins and lots of iron in the menses fluid, the perfect nutrients for bacterial growth. The longer the tampon was worn, the more menses fluid and the more nutrients. You could not have designed a better bed for that bacterial growth if you tried. You were basically inserting a culture medium in the vagina.[12]

In addition, medical experts believe that the tampon's super absorbency caused it to absorb not just menstrual fluids, but also normal vaginal fluids that keep the vaginal walls from drying out. Woman's health expert Nancy Friedman explains: "The range of blood loss during menstruation is two to six ounces. A single super absorbent tampon is capable of soaking up to an ounce or more of fluid. Since menstruation is a gradual process lasting three to seven days, the question arises: If the tampon has absorbed all the blood leaving the uterus and still hasn't reached saturation, what will it absorb? The answer, normal secretions of the healthy vaginal walls."[13]

Dry vaginal walls are easily irritated. They can receive tiny scratches when a tampon rubs against them as well as when a tampon is inserted or removed. Moreover, bits of cellulose tend to stick to dry vaginal walls, thus causing even more damage when the tampon is removed. Indeed, some women reported pain upon removing the new tampons due to dryness. What is more, women who used super absorbent tampons when their level of flow did not necessitate it were almost certain to have abnormal dryness.

Compounding the problem is the fact that placing any device inside the vagina changes the level of acidity in those tissues. The vagina is normally acidic, but menstruation and the use of tampons both lower acidity. The longer a tampon is worn, the sharper the decline in acidity, and this decline is accompanied by a corresponding rise in alkalinity. Extended use, combined with the cellulose in the new tampons, which was treated with an alkali solution that could leach out into the vagina, intensified this change from acid to alkaline. Not surprisingly, *S. aureus* requires an alkali environment in order to grow and produce toxins. Gordon Flynn, professor of pharmacology at the University of Michigan, Ann Arbor, explains: "The tampon had the ability to make the vaginal surface alkaline, which would lead to bacterial colonization and infection."[14]

One Step Forward, but the Mystery Remains

Based on statistical evidence and the theory implicating super-absorbent tampons, the CDC concluded that although the

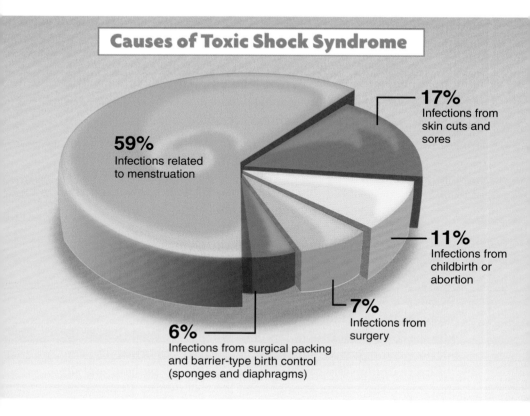

Causes of Toxic Shock Syndrome

17%
Infections from skin cuts and sores

59%
Infections related to menstruation

11%
Infections from childbirth or abortion

7%
Infections from surgery

6%
Infections from surgical packing and barrier-type birth control (sponges and diaphragms)

tampons themselves did not cause TSS, they were a key factor in its development. Manufacturers voluntarily removed the new tampons from the market and ceased using the polyester-cellulose combination in tampon construction.

Nevertheless, much about TSS remains a mystery. Although with the removal of the tampons the number of TSS cases in the United States decreased significantly, TSS did not disappear entirely. For example, in the period from 1980–1981, TSS struck ten in every one hundred thousand Americans. By 2005, that number fell to between two and five per one hundred thousand.

According to the CDC, moreover, approximately 59 percent of all reported cases of TSS are menstrual related. Experts do not know why these cases develop, but hypothesize that failure to change tampons frequently encourages bacterial growth in susceptible individuals. Of the remaining 41 percent of TSS cases, 18 percent occur due to infections caused by surgical procedures. In these cases, the illness develops as a result of infected open wounds and compromised immune systems. Of these, 11 percent occur in women after childbirth or abortions, both of which cause small breaks in the vaginal walls. Another 17 percent of TSS cases occur due to nonsurgical skin lesions such as abscesses and open sores. The remaining 6 percent of nonmenstrual cases have been connected to barrier contraceptives such as diaphragms and contraceptive sponges as well as to surgical packing. Scientists speculate that barrier contraceptive devices and surgical packing keep bacteria close to the body and provide a moist environment conducive to bacterial growth in susceptible individuals. Additionally, surgical packing traps body fluids that the bacteria needs to grow. Hoffman explains: "As with the tampon, surgical packing provides a matrix that soaks up protein-rich fluids, which means the bacteria has food."[15]

Clearly, there is still a lot of mystery surrounding TSS. However, by studying individual cases and establishing links between them, scientists learned enough about the illness to eliminate the threat of an epidemic. Moreover, fewer new cases are reported, and fatalities have been reduced. Although no one knows for sure why cases and fatalities have declined, most experts think that the elimination of the super-absorbent tampons is a key factor.

CHAPTER TWO

Overactivating the Immune System

Most individuals who develop TSS become extremely ill. This happens because the bacteria that cause TSS release toxins that confuse and overactivate the immune system. As a result, the immune system launches an attack on healthy body cells, which causes serious damage to the body.

Invisible Microorganisms

Bacteria are microorganisms too small to be seen with the naked eye. They are found everywhere, including in and on the human body. Some types of bacteria help the body to function by taking up space that would otherwise serve as colonization sites for more dangerous bacteria. Such bacteria are found on the skin, in the digestive and respiratory tracts, and in a woman's reproductive tract.

Other forms of bacteria, however, produce toxins that attack and destroy host tissues, converting them into nutrients for bacterial growth. *Staphylococcus aureus* falls into this group.

Neutralizing Antibodies

About one-quarter of the population carry small quantities of *S. aureus* on their skin and/or in the mucous membranes that line the respiratory, digestive, and female reproductive tracts. In most cases, these bacterial colonies are relatively harmless, or benign. Many, for example, are too small for the bacteria to do any damage. And, because *S. aureus* is not a good competitor with other bacteria, it is unable to displace helpful bacteria in order to gain a stronghold from which to grow. These benign colonies do not become dangerous unless an initiating event,

The bacteria *Staphylococcus aureus*, shown here in a microscopic photograph, can lead to toxic shock syndrome.

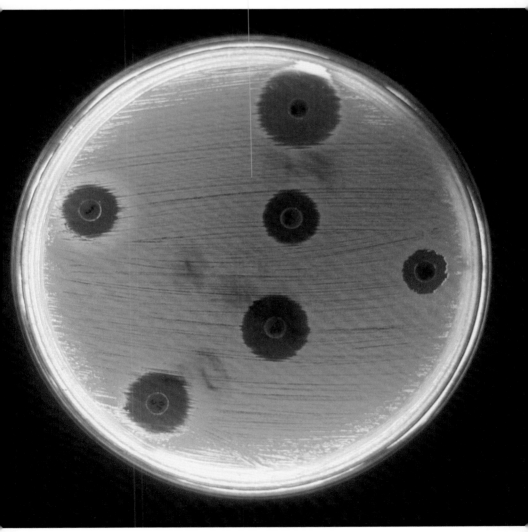

Staph Infections

Besides causing TSS, a strain of *S. aureus* is responsible for a group of skin diseases known as staph infections, which usually enter the body through a break in a person's skin.

Such infections are usually localized, like boils, but sometimes they spread throughout the body. Scalded skin syndrome, which most often affects children under the age of five, starts as a localized staph infection. It produces toxins that allow it to spread and affect the skin all over the body. Scalded skin syndrome causes fever, a rash, and blisters that have the same effect on a person as a serious burn.

Staph infections are highly contagious. The bacteria can be spread through the air, from contact with contaminated surfaces, and from person to person. Individuals can also carry staph bacteria from one area of their body to another. For instance, people can transmit *S. aureus* from their nose onto their fingers and then to a cut or scratch on their arm. It can also pass between people in the same manner, which is why outbreaks are common in places where a large number of people come in close contact. This includes prisons, nursing homes, day care centers, and hospitals, as well as among athletes involved in contact sports like football and wrestling. Hand washing is one of the best ways to keep from being infected.

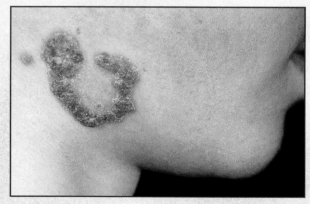

Staphylococcus aureus, which causes TSS, can produce staph infections on the skin like this one.

such as the presence of a surgical wound, causes the colonies to overgrow and secrete toxins. Even if this occurs, because there are many different strains, or kinds, of *S. aureus*, the type, number, and virulence of the toxins the bacteria secrete vary, which impacts the effect on the body. The strain of *S. aureus* that causes TSS, however, produces as many as twenty extremely harmful toxins. Among these are seven lethal toxins known as superantigens. Of these, four are the most likely to lead to TSS. They are TSST-1 and *Staphylococcus aureus* enterotoxins A, B, and C (SEA, SEB, and SEC).

Fortunately, most people produce proteins that attack antigens and superantigens. These proteins, called antibodies, are manufactured by the immune system in response to the presence of foreign substances. Humans produce millions of different antibodies, shaped at the tip to match the molecular structure of a particular antigen. This design, which is similar to a lock and key, makes it possible for the antibody to recognize, attach to, engulf, and destroy its antigen match.

For the body to produce a particular antibody, it must have previously been exposed to the antigen. Thus, people who have never been exposed to a given antigen do not carry antibodies specific to it. At least 80 percent of the population do have antibodies for the superantigens, however, so TSS cases are relatively rare. Hoffman explains: "A person's immunity or antibody production is an important factor. Most people do not get toxic shock syndrome, and the reason is their immune system produces antibodies that are able to wipe out the superantigens."[16]

Medical Emergency

TSS is a medical emergency because individuals who do not produce the proper antibodies cannot defend themselves against the superantigens. If conditions arise that stimulate the overgrowth of *S. aureus*, there is no way to prevent the superantigens from flooding the victim's bloodstream. When the immune system then overreacts, secreting a disproportionately large amount of harmful chemicals that damage the body, the symptoms of TSS appear. New Mexico State

University microbiologist and *S. aureus* expert Dr. John E. Gustafson explains:

> If a person does not produce antibodies to the superantigen(s) elicited by the infected *S. aureus* strain, they then are prone to toxic shock syndrome. For instance, you can have a patient who is infected with a strain of *S. aureus* that produces SEB or SEC. If their body has never seen one or both of these superantigens, they don't have an appropriate immune response to the toxin(s). Therefore, they become very, very sick because the toxin(s) is not removed from their blood.[17]

Breaking Barriers

Before serious problems can occur, one or another of the superantigens must somehow get into an individual's blood. Normally, a tight network of cells in the skin and mucous membranes acts as a barrier to antigens. *S. aureus*, however, produces an enzyme known as hyaluronidase, which erodes this network. It does this by breaking down hyaluronic acid, a substance that bonds the connective tissues of the skin and mucous membranes tightly together. When the connections between the cells loosen, the skin and mucous membrane are vulnerable to breakage. Minor events that ordinarily would not cause a break in the cell wall, such as an individual lightly scratching a sore or a tampon gently rubbing against a vaginal wall, are more likely to produce microscopic scratches that provide the bacteria with a portal of entry into the body. Moreover, *S. aureus* continues secreting hyaluronidase once the bacteria enters the body. Here, hyaluronidase breaks down internal tissues, which makes it easier for toxins to gain access into the bloodstream.

Inhibiting the Attack

As soon as the immune system detects the presence of *S. aureus*, it launches a defense in which white blood cells are sent forth to engulf and destroy any foreign substances. However,

The Immune Response

Immune System Response and the *Staphylococcus Aureus* Bacterium

Immune System Gears Up

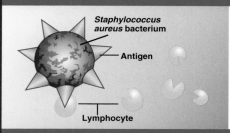

Staphylococcus aureus bacterium

Antigen

Lymphocyte

* The surfaces of bacteria carry markers called antigens, which enable lymphocytes (white blood cells that produce antibodies) to identify them.

* Each lymphocyte recognizes a specific bacterium, just as a key fits a lock.

Normal Immune Response

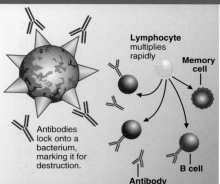

Lymphocyte multiplies rapidly

Memory cell

Antibodies lock onto a bacterium, marking it for destruction.

B cell

Antibody

* When lymphocytes recognize bacteria by their antigens, they divide repeatedly, producing memory cells and B cells.

* Memory cells memorize the antigens, so that the body can react quickly in any future invasion.

* B cells produce chemicals called antibodies, which target new invaders, locking onto their antigens. In this way, they disable the invading bacteria.

Immune System Goes Awry

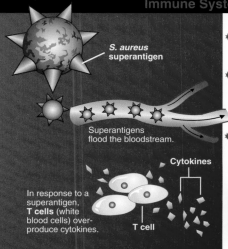

S. aureus superantigen

Superantigens flood the bloodstream.

Cytokines

In response to a superantigen, **T cells** (white blood cells) over-produce cytokines.

T cell

* Some lethal strains of *S. aureus*, called superantigens, produce deadly toxins.

* In people who have never been exposed to the superantigen—and thus do not produce the proper antibodies—the bacteria flood the victim's bloodstream.

* The immune system then overreacts, secreting excessive amounts of chemicals, including cytokines, which damage the body and cause TSS.

> **TSS symptoms are caused by the overreaction of the immune system in response to the superantigen-induced toxins.**

White Blood Cells

White blood cells are really a group of different cells that work together to destroy pathogens. Each type of white blood cell has a specific job.

Neutrophils are the most common type of white blood cells. Neutrophils release a chemical that kills bacteria and foreign substances. Dead neutrophils turn into pus, which macrophages clean up.

Eosinophils and basophils are less common. Eosinophils attack parasites in the skin and the lungs. Basophils are involved in causing inflammation.

Lymphocytes, which become B cells and T cells, focus on viruses and bacteria. B cells produce antibodies. T cells have a variety of jobs. Killer T cells detect and destroy viruses and bacteria. Helper and suppressor T cells control killer T cells, thereby controlling the immune response.

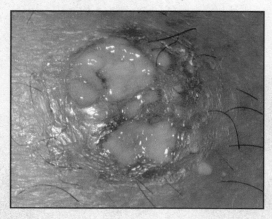

Infections like this one (left) caused by *Staphylococcus aureus* will be attacked by white blood cells, including those below.

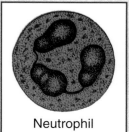

Neutrophil

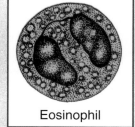

Eosinophil

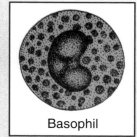

Basophil

hyaluronidase is not the only powerful chemical *S. aureus* emits. It has other secretions that protect the bacteria by confusing and weakening the body's defenses.

Coagulase is one of these substances. It is a protein that stimulates the production of fibrin, a chemical that forms a network of fibers that trap blood cells, thereby creating a blood clot. When *S. aureus* secretes coagulase, a protective network of fibrin forms around the bacteria. Fibrin camouflages the invader, making it difficult for the immune system's marauding white blood cells to identify the bacteria as a foreign substance. The white blood cells that do attack then encounter the protective wall of fibrin encasing the *S. aureus*. As a result, the attack on the bacteria is weakened.

Making matters worse, excess coagulase is sent into the bloodstream. Here, it stimulates the formation of blood clots throughout the body. If a clot forms in an artery or vein, blood flow may be hindered. In severe cases of TSS, blood supply to the feet and hands, which are difficult for the circulatory system to reach under normal conditions, is often reduced.

Without adequate oxygen and nutrition, healthy cells in the fingers, toes, hands, and feet can become gangrenous, which means they die and begin to decompose. In this condition, called gangrene, the affected body part becomes progressively darker, swollen, cold, and numb.

Left untreated, gangrene spreads and can be fatal. Often, the only way to save the patient is to amputate the affected body parts. That is what happened to Jean, a TSS survivor, whose toes were amputated in order to save her life. An article on the Alice Kilvert Tampon Alert Web site, a British organization dedicated to educating the public about TSS, explains that when Jean was admitted to the hospital, "the doctors noticed that the tips of her fingers and toes were turning black with gangrene. . . . The gangrene spread to her knee, nose, and the back of her head."[18]

And if this is not bad enough, if abnormal fibrin production goes unchecked, shortages of the clotting agent arise. When

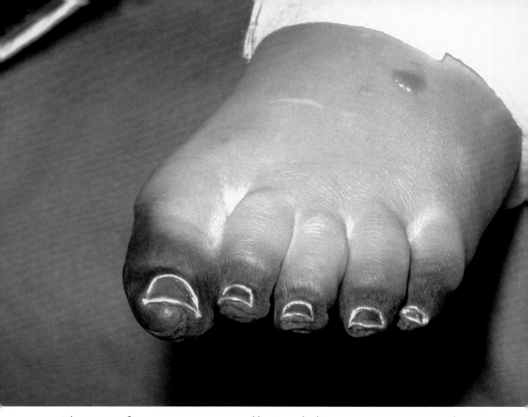

This case of gangrene was caused by *Staphylococcus aureus*. Starved of oxygen and nutrition, the tissue is decomposing.

this happens, damaged organs cannot heal, and internal bleeding, another potentially lethal event, occurs.

More Problems

The ability of *S. aureus* to weaken and confound the immune system does not end here. *S. aureus* produces a toxin known as leukocidin, which attaches to the walls of white blood cells, causing their deaths. In addition, the bacteria secrete sugar molecules known as polysaccharides that coat the bacteria. Many normal cells are also coated with the same substance. The immune system is capable of producing antibodies that can engulf foreign polysaccharides, thereby destroying the bacteria underneath. However, since the polysaccharide coating that forms around *S. aureus* is the same as that which coats normal cells, these antibodies are not released, and the bacteria are protected.

Another chemical known as protein A protects *S. aureus* against antibodies specific to the bacteria. It does this by binding to the wrong end of *S. aureus* antibodies. Each end of an antibody has a particular job. One end activates an immune response, while the other stops such action. Protein A binds to the deactivation end, thus deterring the antibody from doing its job. Gustafson explains: "If you have an antibody against *S. aureus* once protein A binds to it, you get no further activation of the immune response. By binding to the wrong end, protein A effectively inhibits the immune response to *S. aureus*."[19]

Left uncontrolled, *S. aureus* produces still more toxins. One, called hemolysin, lyses, or breaks apart oxygen carrying red blood cells throughout the body. Iron from inside the red blood cells is transported back to the bacteria, providing it with nutrition. When the number of red blood cells is reduced, so too is the level of oxygen that the organs receive. This causes toxic shock patients to feel weak, fatigued, and light-headed. That is what happened to Gina, who was stricken with TSS in 2001. She recalls: "I suddenly felt sick, dizzy, and extremely weak. I said that I'd have to go home to bed as I could hardly stand up."[20]

In this electron micrograph of *Staphylococcus aureus*, protective sticky polysaccharides can be seen wrapped around some of the bacteria.

Two other toxins, known as exfoliative toxins, attack the
skin by impairing a protein whose job it is to keep the outer
layer of the skin whole. As a result, the top layer of skin is
loosened. When the skin is rubbed, no matter how lightly, it
peels off. The skin underneath is red and moist, making an affected individual look like he or she has a severe sunburn, a
characteristic of TSS. Jamie Z., who was diagnosed with TSS
in 2002, describes her experience: "My face had turned bright
red, like I had a really bad sunburn. The doctor looked worried and asked my parents if we had recently been on vacation
in the sun. As soon as my mom said no, the doctor . . . suspected I had TSS."[21]

These scientists are conducting research on the immune system. The
symptoms of toxic shock syndrome result from an overreaction of
the immune system.

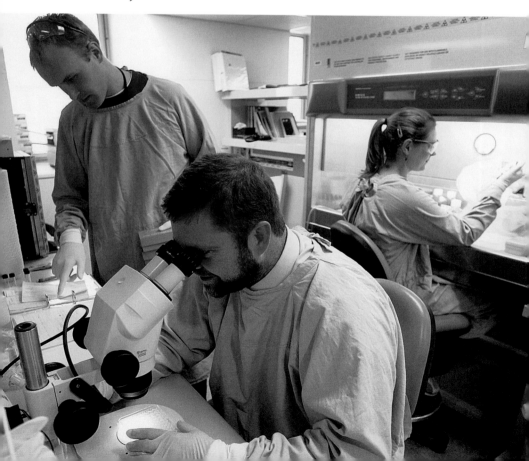

The Immune System Overreacts

Among the immune system's defenses are white blood cells called T cells, which act like the master controls of the immune system. Ordinarily, when T cells come in contact with an antigen, the antigen binds to an area on the T cell called a receptor. This activates the T cell to release into the bloodstream proteins known as cytokines. Cytokines produce inflammation, an immune response that brings about reactions like fever, vomiting, and the dilation of small blood vessels, all of which help the body fight infection.

Cytokines are powerful chemicals, and in excessive amounts they can cause serious damage to the body. Normally, this does not happen: T cells produce limited amounts of cytokines because only one T cell out of thousands is activated when an antigen binds to a T-cell receptor. When superantigens are present, however, they do not bind to the usual T-cell receptor. Instead, they bind to another site on the T cell, causing T cells to overreact wildly.

Stimulation of T cells by a superantigen can induce activation of 20 to 50 percent of all the body's millions of T cells, with corresponding overproduction of cytokines. The result is dangerously high levels of inflammatory response. Gustafson explains: "Let's say ten thousand T cells come in contact with an antigen. Of these ten thousand, one or two are going to be activated and elicit an immune response. But when you have a superantigen, because of the binding site, a plethora of T cells are activated."[22]

Cytokines, the Real Culprit

When a person's system is flooded with cytokines, rather than helping the body fight infection, these chemicals blow the immune response out of proportion. Thus, it is not *S. aureus* or the many toxins it produces that cause the symptoms of TSS, it is the action of the body's own cytokines. For example, cytokines stimulate the brain to set the body's temperature higher, producing fever. This is done as a defense against bacteria, which thrive at normal body temperature but weaken if

As a response to TSS, the immune system produces proteins called cytokines, which cause symptoms such as sudden vomiting.

the temperature rises. However, excess cytokines cause the temperature to rise to dangerous levels. For instance, the flu may cause a person's body temperature to climb to about 100–101°F (37–38°C). It is not uncommon for individuals with TSS to run a fever as high as 105°F (40°C). High fever leads to a rapid pulse and breathing rate as well as severe dehydration, which is characterized by weakness, excess thirst, inability to urinate, mental confusion, and even hallucinations. Jamie Z. recalls: "I started acting really weird. I don't remember much, but my mom said I was talking nonsense and mumbling. Like, at one point, I said to her, 'I need to go to the restaurant to pick up my tips.' My mom looked at me strangely because I didn't waitress anywhere—my high fever was making me delirious! . . . By that point, my temperature had reached 105 [°F (41°C)]."[23]

Cytokines activate other defenses. In an effort to rid the body of toxins, cytokines signal the brain to direct the gastrointestinal system to expel its contents in the form of vomiting and diarrhea. Once again, at normal levels these actions help the body drive out poisons. But when too many cytokines are released, bouts of vomiting and diarrhea become uncontrollable. That was what happened to TSS victim Sue Myers. According to Riley, "She remembers having to throw up in the sink because she was sitting on the toilet and having diarrhea at the same time."[24] Repeated episodes of diarrhea and vomiting, especially in combination with high fever, result in severe dehydration.

In dehydration, loss of water from the blood makes it difficult for the heart to pump enough blood through the body. This, alone, leads to shock. But excess cytokines initiate another defense mechanism that worsens the situation. Cytokines signal small blood vessels throughout the body to dilate, or expand. This process, known as vasodilation, enables blood plasma, the liquid part of the blood that carries antibodies, to pass rapidly through usually narrow capillaries in order to reach surrounding tissues, which may harbor bacteria. When the capillaries are excessively dilated, however, plasma rushes through them and pools in surrounding tissues, leaving less blood in the center of the body for the heart to pump to the organs. Rose, a registered nurse, explains: "Normally, the capillaries are contracted. Due to vasodilation, they expand until their carrying capacity is huge. Blood that normally circulates throughout the body is basically sucked up into the capillaries and there is not enough blood to go around."[25]

Shock

As a result of reduced circulation as well as loss of fluid in the blood, blood pressure drops. Blood pressure is created as the heart pumps blood into the arteries, making the artery walls expand. The less blood the heart has to pump, the lower the pressure.

Blood pressure is measured in millimeters and stated as two numbers. For example, normal blood pressure is about 120/80. The top number signifies the pressure exerted as the heart contracts, and the bottom number indicates the pressure when the heart relaxes. TSS can cause an individual's blood pressure to drop so low that it cannot be measured with a blood pressure cuff. "My blood pressure was extremely low," Jamie Z. reports, "around 50 over 20."[26]

With low blood pressure, the heart can pump only slowly and with less force than it normally does. Thus, less blood is pumped to the body. The vital organs become starved for the oxygen and nutrients that the blood delivers. As a result, they cannot function properly. If normal blood pressure is not reestablished, the body goes into shock. According to microbiologists Abigail Salyers and Dixie D. Whitt, "Shock is a clinical term used to describe a set of events that lead to the collapse of the circulatory system and can result in multiple organ failure and death."[27]

Shock is characterized by confusion, weakness, dizziness, a rapid pulse rate caused by the heart beating faster in an attempt to raise the blood pressure, and rapid breathing, which is the body's way to draw more oxygen into the bloodstream. If shock is not treated, lack of blood can cause multiple organs to fail. Once this occurs, death is inevitable.

Fast Work

What makes the course of TSS even more threatening is the timing. Once a superantigen enters the bloodstream, shock and organ failure can occur in six hours. As Leslie puts it, "One day you're perfectly fine and the next day you're deathly ill."[28]

Behind this fast work is the strain of *S. aureus* that causes TSS to grow up to ten thousand times faster than other strains

Victims of toxic shock syndrome become sick very quickly.

of the pathogen. In less than an hour's time, millions of new bacteria are created, and these flood the body with enormous quantities of superantigens. To put this in perspective, in animal studies conducted at the University of Minnesota Medical School, Minneapolis, in the 1980s, a single milligram of the superantigen TSST-1 elicited an immune response that could have killed a 220 pound (99.79kg) person. As much as 10 milligrams of the toxin have been found in the bloodstream of patients who died from TSS.

Clearly, TSS is a dangerous illness. The ability of *S. aureus* to grow rapidly allows it to produce great amounts of toxins, including superantigens. These weaken, confuse, and overactivate the immune system. This causes a massive inflammatory response, which, if uncontrolled, rapidly leads to shock, organ failure, and death. Fortunately, if treatment is administered in a timely fashion, the damaging effects of TSS can be lessened.

CHAPTER THREE

A Medical Emergency

Diagnosing TSS is difficult. The initial symptoms are easily mistaken for a number of other illnesses. Cell cultures and blood samples can reveal the presence of *Staphylococcus aureus* and toxins, but laboratory analysis takes time, and death from TSS can occur in a matter of hours. Therefore, TSS is considered a medical emergency, calling for immediate treatment. Indeed, treatment often begins before laboratory test results are completed.

Confusing Symptoms

Not every patient exhibits all the symptoms associated with TSS. For instance, people with TSS may not have a rash if exfoliative toxins have not yet been released into their bloodstream. Their body temperature may not reach abnormally high levels until cytokines flood their bodies. Moreover, blood pressure may not drop significantly until capillary dilation and/or severe dehydration has occurred. Medical writer Dixie Farley explains: "Not all cases are exactly alike, and you may not have all the symptoms. You may have aching muscles, bloodshot eyes, or a sore throat. . . . The sunburn-like rash may not develop until you're very ill; it may go unnoticed if it's only on a small area."[29]

Complicating matters even further, the initial symptoms of TSS mimic those of a wide range of other illnesses. As in TSS, most of these conditions are characterized by inflammation, which is the body's way of fighting infection no matter the

Symptoms of Toxic Shock Syndrome

Toxic shock syndrome typically starts with a wide range of symptoms, which can appear at any time in cases of nonmenstrual TSS but always begins after a period starts in menstrual TSS. Common symptoms include sudden high fever; chills; fatigue; aching muscles; sore throat; headache; abdominal pain; red eye; nausea; vomiting; diarrhea; a sunburn-like rash on the abdomen, chest, or thigh; peeling skin; confusion; dizziness; fainting or feeling faint; and thirst. Left unchecked, these symptoms lead to low blood pressure, shock, organ failure, and death.

TSS symptoms do not always occur simultaneously. In some cases, only one or two may occur. The number and severity depend on how far the condition has progressed. The more virulent the superantigens, the stronger the inflammatory response and the more severe the symptoms.

Toxic Shock Syndrome Symptoms

- ☑ Sudden high fever
- ☑ Vomiting
- ☑ Sunburn-like rash
- ☑ Diarrhea
- ☑ Fainting or feeling faint
- ☑ Muscle aches
- ☑ Dizziness
- ☑ Confusion

infecting pathogen. For example, fever, headaches, a sore throat, muscle aches, weakness, and fatigue typify the flu as well as measles, scarlet fever, and Rocky Mountain spotted fever, which are also characterized by a red rash. Stomach viruses, food poisoning, and appendicitis share many of these same symptoms plus diarrhea and vomiting. Because of similarities, the early symptoms of TSS are often confused with other conditions. A case study on the Web site Alice Kilvert Tampon Alert describes what happened to Delyse:

> On Saturday morning, Delyse suddenly started vomiting, had severe diarrhea and a high temperature. She thought she was suffering from food poisoning. Later that day her partner called the doctor, who diagnosed flu. On Monday, Delyse went back to the GP [general practioner] who diagnosed gastritis [inflammation of the lining of the stomach]. Her condition worsened and on Tuesday she was admitted to the local hospital with a suspected burst appendix.[30]

Delyse died five weeks later on September 9, 1993.

Diagnostic Tests

Because TSS symptoms are so easily confused with a multitude of other conditions, the initial physical examination should include the taking of blood samples as well as cell cultures from the patient's vagina, if menstrual toxic shock is suspected, or from skin sores. These are sent to a laboratory, where trained specialists examine them under a microscope. Different pathogens can be identified by their size, shape, and the way they move. Toxins are hard to detect, but blood samples often reveal them indirectly by showing evidence of antibodies to a particular toxin. Test results allow physicians to rule out other conditions.

Unfortunately, since time is of the essence in combating superantigens, physicans do not have the luxury of waiting for hours for test results before treating TSS patients. Therefore,

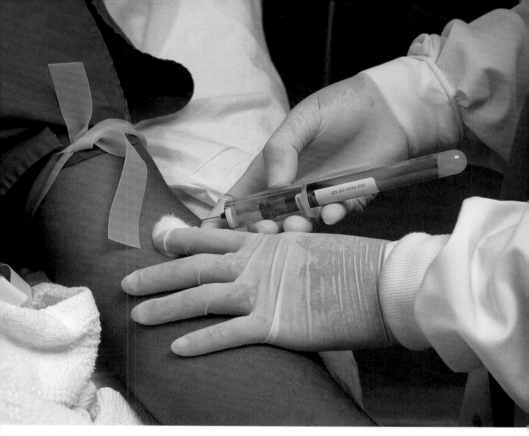

Doctors will usually take a blood sample from a patient suffering from TSS-like symptoms.

medical professionals examine risk factors that make an individual susceptible to TSS in order to make a tentative diagnosis. If any of these factors can be linked to the patient, TSS is considered and treatment for the condition is administered even before an official diagnosis is made. This prevents treatment delays, which might lead to organ failure. Dr. Jacques Carter of Boston's Beth Israel Deaconess Medical Center explains:

> Most of the symptoms of TSS can also be caused by other conditions or diseases, such as Rocky Mountain spotted fever and measles. However, when a high fever and a number of other symptoms associated with TSS suddenly strike during or soon after a woman's menstrual period, doctors generally suspect TSS and begin treatment while

simultaneously searching to see if another condition or disease is the underlying cause.[31]

Once laboratory results are in, if a misdiagnosis has been made, the treatment is altered to suit the official diagnosis. Since most of the conditions that mimic TSS are not usually life threatening, treating for TSS rather than the flu, for example, does less harm to the patient than the reverse.

Looking at Risk Factors

There are a number of risk factors that medical professionals look for when diagnosing TSS. Gender is important. All menstrual TSS cases and about 75 percent of nonmenstrual cases

Women who have just given birth are at greater risk of contracting TSS. *Staphylococcus aureus* can enter the vaginal wall through microabrasions caused during delivery.

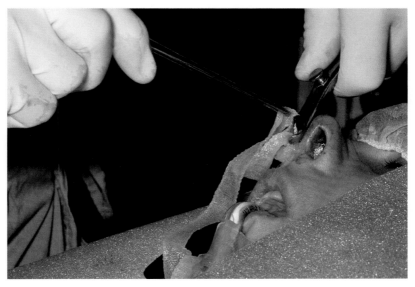

Nasal surgery patients like this one are at risk of developing TSS due to the absorbent packing placed in the nose, where colonies of *Staphylococcus aureus* are common.

occur in females. Moreover, females who have recently given birth, had an abortion, or used barrier contraceptives are at risk. These events can cause microabrasions to the vaginal walls, which provide *S. aureus* a portal of entry.

Menstruation is another key factor. More than half of all reported instances of TSS occur in menstruating females. Prolonged use of tampons also sends up a red flag, as does a patient's youth. Teenagers whose immune systems are not fully developed may not have built up antibodies against *S. aureus* and/or the superantigens. About 41 percent of all menstrual TSS cases occur in females between the ages of thirteen and nineteen.

For the same reason, young children who have had nonsurgical wounds are at risk of developing nonmenstrual TSS, with more than half of such cases affecting children under two years of age. In fact, a Wisconsin study published in the *Journal of Infectious Diseases* in October 1983 compared the presence of antibodies specific to TSS toxins in stored blood plasma obtained from 689 mixed-age subjects. The investigators found the antibodies in 47 percent of the one-year-old subjects, whereas 88 percent of the twenty-year-old subjects had these immune system proteins.

Recent surgical procedures also put individuals at risk. Following surgery, patients often have weakened immune systems and/or infected or open wounds. Nasal surgery patients are especially imperiled. The nose is a traditional site for *S. aureus* colonies, and absorbent packing placed in the nose after surgery appears to encourage bacterial growth. Dr. Ferhat Erisir, an Istanbul University specialist in problems in the nose and throat, has cited an incidence of TSS after nasal surgery of sixteen for every one hundred thousand patients. Other patients with weakened immune systems that cannot easily fight off the effects of *S. aureus* are also at risk. These include individuals infected by HIV, cancer, and diabetes, as well as individuals who undergo frequent kidney dialysis. Indeed, dialysis patients not only have weakened immune systems, but because the procedure involves needle punctures to the skin, they also often have open wounds that provide the bacteria a portal of entry.

In addition, individuals who have had TSS in the past are in danger. One-third of all TSS sufferers report recurrences usually within six months of the first episode. Although it would seem that TSS survivors should develop protective antibodies after being exposed to a superantigen, this does not seem to occur. Rather, the body of a person who has had TSS becomes more sensitive to TSS. Scientists do not know why this is so. They speculate that a genetic mutation may reduce the ability of certain people to produce the proper protective antibodies. This makes for susceptiblity to TSS.

A Medical Emergency

If consideration of a patient's symptoms and risk factors leads to a tentative diagnosis of TSS, the physician begins treatment. The main goal is to reverse the effects of shock and stop organ failure. Such treatment usually begins in a hospital emergency room, where medical professionals perform a number of specialized procedures on the patient.

Counteracting the effects of dehydration is the first and most important step medical professionals take to reverse shock. Patients are connected to at least one, and often multiple, intravenous drips, which restore lost fluids and electrolytes directly to the bloodstream in large amounts. According to the Toxic Shock Information Service, an organization dedicated to researching TSS and educating health care professionals and the public about the condition, dehydration can be so severe that an adult TSS patient can require as much as 2.6 gallons of fluid (10l) in the first twenty-four hours of treatment. In comparison,

Patients tentatively diagnosed with TSS are usually taken to the emergency room, where they receive fluids, oxygen, antibiotics, and other medications.

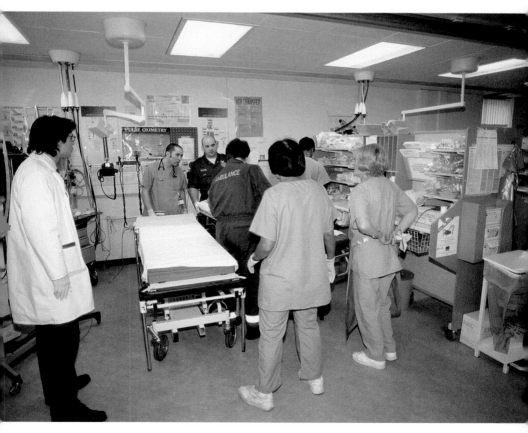

postsurgical patients require 3.17 quarts of fluids (3l) in the same time period. Replacing lost fluids helps raise the patient's blood pressure, thereby improving blood circulation.

At the same time, oxygen is administered through an oxygen mask. This helps the patient breathe more easily and increases the supply of oxygen in the bloodstream. To help oxygen reach the brain, patients are laid down with their legs propped up about 12 inches (30.48cm) high. Nurse Lois Sterenchuk describes the hectic scene in the emergency room when TSS patient Pat Kehm was brought in:

> The doctors were ordering many intravenous fluids and trying to expand her fluid volume. . . . There were two trauma nurses there all the time I was there, two or three ambulance people were there, and they were assisting getting things that were being asked for, IV solutions, the nurses were monitoring her blood pressure, were fixing medications, hanging IVs, providing oxygen, monitoring Pat's other vital signs, puncturing an artery to withdraw blood and sending to the lab for tests and discussing why her pressure wouldn't come up.[32]

While this is going on, medical personnel try to identify the site of bacterial growth. Once it is established, steps are taken to decontaminate it. Thus, any tampon, barrier contraceptive, or surgical packing is removed. Sores, wounds, and burns are disinfected, and pus is drained out.

In addition, dead and damaged tissue and foreign material are removed from infected wounds. In this procedure, called debridement, a surgeon uses a scalpel to carve away at infected areas in and around a wound. Debridement helps eliminate, or at least reduce, bacterial colonies, which, in turn, decreases toxin production. Moreover, by removing dead and damaged tissue that has been stimulating inflammation, the procedure lessens the inflammatory response. Wounds are usually debrided until they bleed heavily, to flood the infected area with protective antibodies.

Medications

A number of medications are administered intravenously. Each serves a distinct purpose, such as reducing inflammation, raising blood pressure, constricting the capillaries, and inhibiting bacterial growth. For instance, anti-inflammatory drugs like aspirin or ibuprofen are prescribed to reduce inflammation and lower fever. If these drugs do not prove to be potent enough, corticosteroids are administered.

Corticosteroids are synthetic copies of inflammation-fighting hormones found in the body. They stop inflammation entirely by suppressing the immune system. Although this response can be extremely valuable in reducing the damage caused by cytokines, it also stops the release of protective antibodies and makes it easier for secondary infections to develop. Therefore, corticosteroids are only used when less powerful medications fail to reduce inflammation significantly.

To raise the person's blood pressure, the vasoconstrictor dopamine may be prescribed. Vasoconstrictors cause the capillaries to narrow, forcing pooled-up blood back to the center of the body.

Although vasoconstrictors can be extremely helpful, they can also have negative effects such as inhibiting the kidneys' ability to function. This can be particularly problematic because the effects of TSS often weaken the kidneys, making them more vulnerable to damage from dopamine. If fluid therapy has produced no rise in an individual's blood pressure, however, dopamine or other vasoconstrictors can save a patient's life.

Antibiotics

Patients are also treated with high doses of antibiotics that destroy *S. aureus*. This therapy can be tricky because some strains of *S. aureus* are resistant to a number of antibiotics. All strains of *S. aureus* are resistant to penicillin; therefore it is no longer prescribed. Problems arise because some strains of *S. aureus* are resistant to multiple antibiotics, such as cephalosporins, tetracyclines, and erythromycins, to name a few. These strains are known as methicillin-resistant *S. aureus* (MRSA, pronounced "mersa").

It is possible for a person to be infected by a nonresistant strain of *S. aureus* that mutates into MRSA once antibiotic treatment begins. Therefore, some patients are treated with four or five different antibiotics which all prove to be ineffective. In these cases, there is only one other drug, vancomycin, which has any effect on the bacteria. Vancomycin is not tried first because

In this electron micrograph, a *Staphylococcus aureus* bacterium that has burst after the application of an antibiotic can be seen above another bacterium that is about to divide.

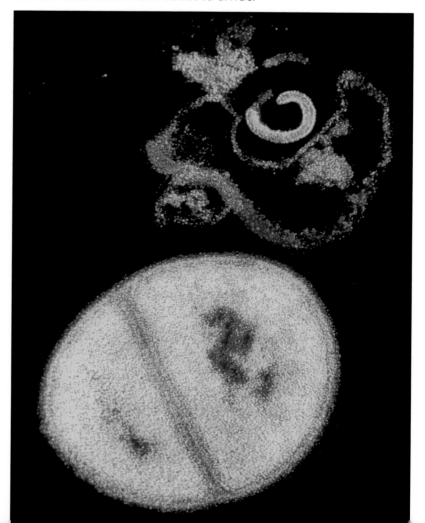

Antibiotic-Resistant Bacteria

Bacterial antibiotic resistance is a natural event. When faced with an anti-infective drug, bacteria mutate in order to survive. This can happen spontaneously due to transformation, a process in which one bacterial cell acquires antibiotic resistance from another.

Once bacteria acquire antibiotic resistance, the bacteria multiply rapidly. Author Ricki Lewis explains: "When a person takes an antibiotic, the drug kills the defenseless bacteria, leaving behind—or 'selecting,' in biological terms—those that can resist it. These renegade bacteria then multiply, increasing their numbers a millionfold in a day, becoming the predominant microorganism." Therefore, treatment with antibiotics, although beneficial, creates a situation in which antibiotic resistance develops.

Ricki Lewis, "The Rise of Antibiotic-Resistant Infections," U.S. Food and Drug Administration. www.fda.gov/fdac/features/795_antibio.html.

when treatment with multiple antibiotics does work, it is more effective against *S. aureus* than vancomycin. A report in a Turkish medical journal describes the effect of treatment with multiple antibiotics combined with dopamine and fluid therapy on a sixteen-year-old boy who developed TSS after nasal surgery: "The patient was treated with intravenous fluid administration and intravenous antibiotic therapy with Cloxacillin and ceftriaxone to provide coverage for TSS. . . . A dopamine drip was also started to maintain blood pressure. The patient improved rapidly and was afebrile [without fever] within 24 hours. . . . The patient was discharged on the fourth day."[33]

Fighting Toxins

Even when antibiotic therapy is effective, it cannot cure TSS. Antibiotics stop bacterial growth, which, in turn, halts new toxin production. But antibiotics do not destroy toxins and superantigens that are already in the bloodstream. In order to fight these toxins, it is necessary to administer immunoglobin intravenously.

Immunoglobin is a blood product that contains plasma—the part of the blood that carries antibodies. The immunoglobin that is used therapeutically comes from plasma collected from thousands of donors and then pooled together. Immunoglobin pooled in this way is more likely to contain antibodies needed to fight the superantigens than plasma from one individual.

Microbiologist Dr. John E. Gustafson explains:

> What we do is we take your antibodies; we take my antibodies; we take Joe, Tom, Dick, and Harry's antibodies and we pool them. As a population we have had quite a chance to come in contact with one of the staphyloccocal superantigens and elicit an immune response. In that pooled collection of immunoglobin there is probably some anti-superantigen antibodies present. By giving that as a therapy, they are adding these antibodies to the patient's blood. The antibodies will then go and bind to the toxins and destroy them.[34]

Blood transfusions may also be necessary. A blood transfusion is the transfer of blood or blood components from a blood donor into the circulatory system of a recipient. Since the blood of TSS patients often lacks sufficient liquid, a blood component called serum albumin, which is the liquid part of the blood, is given. Serum albumin is a plasma derivative, so in addition to bringing the amount of circulatory liquid up to normal levels, a transfusion of serum albumin may also raise the patient's antibody levels. Depending on the patient's condition, multiple blood transfusions may be performed. One TSS survivor reports being given three blood transfusions in an eight-day period.

Careful Monitoring

Once patients are stabilized, they are admitted to the intensive care unit of the hospital, where specially trained health care professionals carefully monitor their condition. Here patients are connected to machines that scrutinize the functions of their vital organs. These machines are linked to monitors in the patient's room and at the nurse's station, so if there is any change in the patient's condition or if organs start to fail, a nurse knows immediately.

Among the most important of these devices for tracking vital functions is a heart monitor, which records the patient's heart rhythm and warns of heart failure. Equally vital is an arterial line, a tube inserted into an artery in the patient's arm at

After initial treatment, toxic shock syndrome patients are generally moved to the intensive care unit, where they can be carefully monitored.

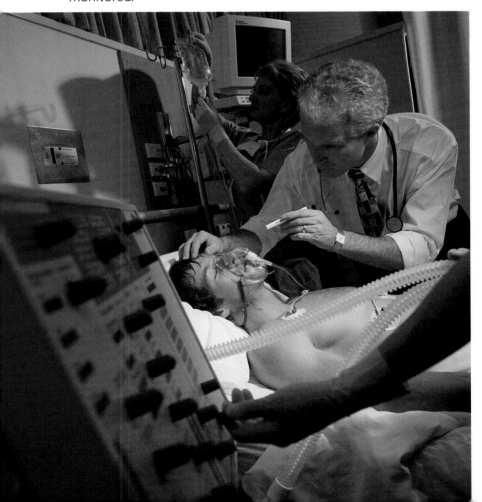

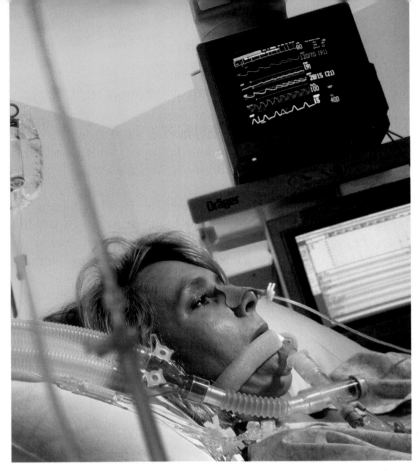

In intensive care, patients are connected to a variety of tubes and sensors that measure vital signs such as blood pressure and kidney function.

one end. At the other it is fitted to a cable attached to a computer that continuously records the patient's blood pressure. Yet another tube is inserted into the patient's bladder. Known as a urinary catheter, this tube serves to drain the bladder and allow hospital staff to measure urinary output. This knowledge helps medical professionals to assess the patient's kidney functions and warns them if that organ seems to be failing.

When Organs Fail

Even with the best of care, when an individual's blood pressure drops drastically, lack of sufficient blood can inhibit the ability of vital organs to function effectively. Special life-support machines such as a respirator and a dialyzer can assist these organs while patients heal.

A respirator is an artificial breathing machine. It is attached to a tube placed down a patient's windpipe that causes the lungs to inflate and deflate automatically, in effect, breathing for the patient. A dialyzer is an artificial kidney that removes from the blood waste that would ordinarily be eliminated through urination. Blood from an artery is pumped through the dialyzer, where waste products are removed. The newly purified blood is returned to the body through a vein.

Just as the name implies, life-support machines are necessary to keep patients alive. Erin, who suffered from TSS in 2003, recalls: "I was on dialysis, on a ventilator [a type of respirator], and on massive doses of antibiotics and other medications to prevent other organ failure. My kidneys, liver and gastrointestinal tract were all out of commission and I had drugs to raise my blood pressure."[35]

Usually, as patients become stronger their need for life-support machines disappears. Since approximately 95 percent of all TSS victims recover, most TSS patients on life support survive. Indeed, Erin was able to go back to work six weeks after being released from the hospital and participated in a walkathon a year later.

With prompt treatment, most patients survive TSS and eventually resume their normal lives. It is clear that diagnosing and treating the condition is complicated and, because TSS constitutes a medical emergency, immediate care is required. In most cases, such care reverses the progress of the illness and prevents fatalities. One TSS survivor, Leslie, is grateful to be alive. "I feel like I owe my recovery to the doctors and nurses in the intensive care unit at [Good Samaritan Hospital, Dayton, Ohio]," she explains. "They watched over me so carefully."[36]

CHAPTER FOUR

Recovery and Prevention

Toxic shock syndrome has a profound effect on the body, and recovery from a severe attack can be a slow process. TSS survivors cope with a variety of problems, not least of which is the threat of a recurrence. The preventive steps individuals take to minimize the threat of recurrence can also help the public avoid developing TSS.

A Difficult Recovery

TSS takes a toll on an individual's body. Even after TSS survivors are released from the hospital, they are usually weak. At best, this means they fatigue easily and are unable to resume their normal activities until their bodies become stronger. This can take anywhere from a few days to a year or more. TSS survivors with organ damage may never regain their previous strength.

Recovery is difficult because the body has been exhausted by the attack of toxins and superantigens and by the overactivation of the immune system. Thus, complaints of overwhelming fatigue are common. "My recovery has been slow," Shakeira, a TSS survivor, explains. "I don't have the same energy."[37]

This lack of energy can be debilitating enough to force people to make changes in their routines to conserve energy. Until they regain their strength, they often cut back on regular activities, reducing work hours, curtailing social activities, and getting help with such tasks as housework and child care.

Stopping and resting whenever they feel tired and taking frequent naps also help individuals to fight fatigue. Indeed, getting adequate sleep not only helps to conserve energy, it also promotes healing. Eating a well-balanced diet also strengthens the body, as does mild exercise. Taking short walks, for example, builds up muscles and increases stamina.

Weak Muscles

Even walking can be a challenge for some individuals recovering from TSS. Many spend at least a week confined to bed, while some spend a month or more, and leg muscles weaken from lack of use. TSS survivors in whom blood clots caused gangrene often have had one or more toes amputated. Since the toes help people maintain their balance, loss of even one toe impacts a person's mobility. Not surprisingly then, when they are first released from the hospital, many TSS victims are

Even after recovery from toxic shock syndrome, patients are often weak and tired for some time.

Inside a Hospital Rehabilitation Unit

A hospital rehabilitation unit is a special section of a hospital designed for patients in need of extensive physical therapy for temporary or permanent physical impairments. Inpatient therapy sessions are exhausting, usually running for about three hours per day, five days a week.

The team of health care professionals that work with rehabilitation unit patients includes a patient's primary care physician, a rehabilitation physician, a physical therapist, and a rehabilitation nurse. This team designs a customized rehabilitation program to meet each patient's individual needs. For TSS patients with weakened muscles and/or amputated toes, the goal of the program is usually to improve mobility.

To achieve this goal, TSS patients are likely to use a tilt table, a piece of equipment that looks like a massage table. The patient is strapped on to the table by three wide straps, and then the therapist presses a button to move the tilt table electronically anywhere from 0 to 90 degrees. The greater the angle, the more weight on the patient's feet.

This woman is undergoing physical rehabilitation, which is necessary for the full recovery of some toxic shock syndrome patients.

unable to walk without assistance. "I was so weak that my dad had to carry me off the plane and had to help me to walk about ten steps,"[38] Lisa, who had TSS, recalls.

Physical therapy helps TSS survivors strengthen their muscles and improve their mobility. Patients who have spent a month or more in ICU, as well as those who have had toes amputated, often start these sessions in the rehabilitation unit of the hospital. Here, physical therapists use specialized equipment to assist patients to put weight gradually on enfeebled limbs. When patients are too weak to do this on their own, the therapist and the equipment move the patient's muscles for them. Lisa, who spent one month in ICU and had the tips of her toes amputated, explains: "I was moved to Rehab. That was probably the hardest part of the whole hospital stay. They started with 'dangling' my feet, then I went to a tilt table [and] eventually to other machines that would allow only very little weight on my feet."[39]

Upon release from the hospital, TSS survivors usually attend physical therapy sessions in a gym-like center with weight training machines, exercise bicycles, pulleys, and massage tables. Under the supervision of a physical therapist, outpatients perform individually customized exercises designed to strengthen their bodies and increase their mobility.

Even with physical therapy, some individuals, such as those who have had multiple toes amputated, may never be able to walk normally. Physical therapy helps them to maximize their mobility, thus providing them with the skills they need to cope. Such skills range from learning how to use a cane or other assistive devices such as special shoes, which facilitate balance and walking, to learning the simplest way to climb stairs. Most TSS survivors, however, do regain full mobility. Lisa recalls:

Many toxic shock syndrome victims have difficulty moving about and require a walker like the one this man is using.

"Since I could barely walk, I was in intense physical therapy for quite a while. Eventually I went from walking with a walker to a cane, and then to nothing at all."[40]

Damaged Organs

TSS survivors with damaged organs face additional challenges. For instance, damage to the lungs can cause fluid to build up inside them. This not only makes breathing difficult, but can be fatal. The lungs may fill up to the extent that the person drowns. Drainage tubes inserted into the lungs solve this problem. If damage to the lungs is severe, the tubes may be left in place for weeks or months after the patient is released from the hospital. These individuals require frequent medical monitoring until the tubes can be removed and the lungs have recovered. That is what happened to Erin. She explains: "I was released from the hospital on September 10th 2003. I still had two drainage tubes in my chest and was incredibly weak. It took me about a year to regain almost full lung capacity."[41]

Similarly, some individuals with serious damage to their kidneys require kidney dialysis during their recovery. Dialysis sessions are held in a special unit of a hospital, in a dialysis center, or in a person's home, for four hours at a time, three times a week. Usually, the need for dialysis disappears as a TSS survivor's kidneys heal. If an individual's kidneys have lost 85 to 90 percent of their normal function, the need for dialysis is permanent.

Skin and Hair Loss

The effects of TSS cause other problems that can temporarily affect an individual's physical appearance. For instance, traces of exfoliative toxins that have not been expelled from the body cause the skin on the palms of TSS survivors' hands and feet to peel off. This is the body's way of ridding itself of these toxins. Skin shedding usually occurs after the patient is released from the hospital and does not end until all vestiges of exfoliative toxins are expelled from the body. During this process, the skin often peels off in sheets or flakes off in a manner similar to sunburned skin.

The under layer of new skin appears red and is tender and sensitive to the touch. Consequently, it is vulnerable to injuries. Simple measures like not going barefoot and wearing protective gloves while housecleaning, gardening, or washing dishes help safeguard vulnerable new skin.

Hair loss is another challenge. Hair follicles form below the skin, where they are fed by blood. When individuals have TSS, the follicles absorb toxins through the bloodstream. As the

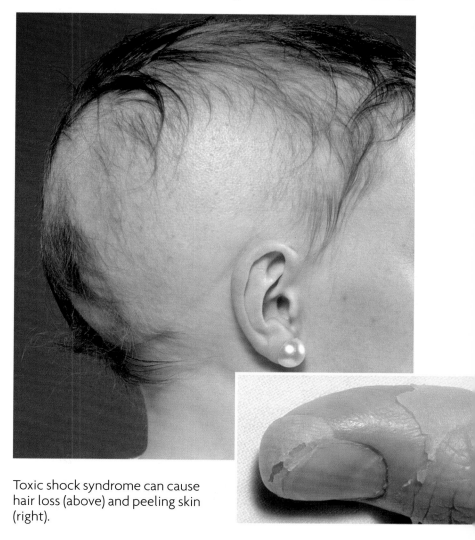

Toxic shock syndrome can cause hair loss (above) and peeling skin (right).

body rids itself of toxins, hair growing in the follicles falls out. Some individuals lose all of the hair on their head as well as hair on their body, while others only lose clumps of hair.

Hair loss is temporary. But until new hair grows in, many individuals wear hats, scarves, caps, wigs, or turbans. Robin, whose classmate developed TSS, recalls:

A girl I went to school with had toxic shock. After she came back to school, all her hair fell out, and the skin on her hands peeled off. It was very strange. She wore a baseball cap and little white gloves every day for the whole semester. The next year when school started she was back to normal; her skin looked okay and her hair had grown back. It was short and curly, just like it had been before she got sick.[42]

Weight Gain or Loss

Because kidney damage makes it difficult to eliminate the extra fluids used in rehydration treatment, some people's weight balloons, making them look bloated and causing unpleasant swelling of different parts of the body. Prolonged treatment with corticosteroids can also lead to fluid retention. Indeed, some individuals gain as many as 50 pounds (22.68kg) in this manner. Leslie was shocked at her appearance. She recalls: "I looked like a monster. I was so fat and puffy."[43] Generally, as damaged kidneys heal or as traces of corticosteroids are eliminated, excess fluid is expelled from the body. Before long, most people return to their normal weight.

Drastic weight loss can also be a challenge. Severe protracted diarrhea, vomiting, and fever rob the body of valuable nutrients and decrease the appetite. These symptoms alone can result in drastic weight loss, and other factors can worsen matters. For example, most people with TSS are too sick to keep food down. Consequently, they are usually fed intravenously in an effort to prevent malnutrition. Although intravenous feeding provides essential nutrients, it, too, often leads to weight loss. And even people who are able to eat normally may experience poor appetite due to their illness or the effects of the different medications coursing through their bodies.

Fortunately, appetites gradually return with healing. Eating frequent small, light meals helps individuals consume sufficient calories before their appetite is robust enough to tolerate three regular meals. Supplementing meals with frequent nutritious snacks, as well as calorie- and nutrient-rich liquids such as smoothies, shakes, and commercially sold liquid food supplements, serves the same purpose. Moderate exercise helps too. It not only increases a person's appetite, but also builds muscle mass, which is often lost or reduced when an individual loses excess weight.

With such measures, people usually return to their normal weight. That is what happened to Lisa. During her hospitalization, she explains, "my weight went all the way down to 82.5 pounds [37.42kg]." As her health improved, so did her appetite. Today, she says: "I am back to my normal weight of about 125 pounds [56.70kg]."[44]

Weakened Immune System

Problems also extend to recovering individuals' immune systems. For a time period ranging anywhere from a few weeks to a few years, many TSS survivors are susceptible to infection. The attack of toxins and superantigens on a TSS victim's body weakens his or her immune system, lessening its ability to fight invading pathogens. Making matters worse, treatment with large doses of antibiotics destroys helpful bacteria as well as pathogens.

Susceptibility varies from person to person. Generally, more severe the case of TSS, the greater and more longer lasting the problem. Four years after developing TSS, Jamie C. is still coping with this challenge. Women's health activist Willi Nolan reports:

Although Jamie has regained much of her former health, she will never be the same. Now, she, her friends and her family have to be incredibly careful about her health. . . . She is still occasionally rushed to the hospital with one or another threatening condition; the last time I heard about, it was mononucleoisis. . . . Jamie has been regularly suffering health problems related to Toxic Shock four years later![45]

In order to keep themselves healthy, TSS survivors take steps to minimize their risk of infection. This involves avoiding people who have been sick as well as areas in which germs can easily spread: Crowded buses, trains, airports, movie theaters, and shopping malls are just a few places.

Other measures that are important for everyone are especially important for people with compromised immune systems. For example, TSS survivors who neglect commonsense

Boosting the Body's Natural Defenses with Herbal Remedies

Some TSS survivors complement their efforts to strengthen their immune system with herbs. Herbs are medicinal plants that have been used for thousands of years for healing. Herbal remedies contain leaves, stems, seeds, and roots of plants with healing properties. They are usually taken ground up in capsule form or as tea. Despite a lack of conclusive testing to prove the effectiveness of herbal remedies, many people take herbal preparations that are believed to stimulate the immune system to help avoid infection.

Among these herbs are echinacea, Siberian ginseng, and garlic. Echinacea is derived from a North American wildflower known as the purple coneflower. Herbalists believe that chemicals in echinacea trigger the production of white blood cells as well as give the herb antibacterial properties.

Siberian ginseng is another choice. Herbalists say it strengthens the body's natural defenses by helping the immune system respond rapidly to infection and counteracting the effects of stress. Usually practices like frequent hand washing are more likely to succumb to infection.

Getting an annual flu shot is another vital step, as is living a healthy lifestyle. Since smoking and abusing alcohol or drugs can depress the immune system, such activities are to be avoided. Exposure to stressful situations should be minimized whenever possible, because stress triggers changes in the immune system that suppress white blood cell production.

In addition, getting eight hours of sleep each night, exercising in moderation, and eating a healthy diet all boost the body's natural defenses. As an extra precaution, some people supplement their diets with a multiple vitamin to ensure they are getting all the nutrients their immune systems need to function efficiently.

taken in tea, Siberian ginseng is a root that some people also add to soups and stews as a way to supercharge their food.

Garlic is an ancient infection fighter. Known to have antibacterial properties, it has been used to ward off infection for thousands of years. In fact, during the mid-1300s plague, healers often wore necklaces made from garlic to protect themselves from developing the disease.

Some people believe that medicinal plants such as ginseng can aid the recovery of toxic shock syndrome survivors.

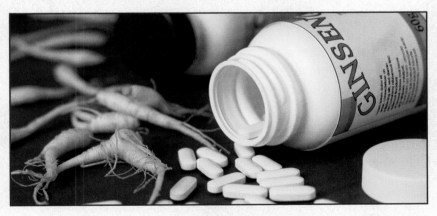

The Threat of Recurrence

Perhaps the most menacing threat TSS survivors face is the possibility of the illness recurring. According to the Toxic Shock Syndrome Information Service of Australia, an organization dedicated to providing information about TSS, "People who have had TSS do not seem to develop immunity as their body cannot build up antibodies to protect them from the toxin."[46]

The threat of recurrence can be both physically and emotionally challenging. Women who have had menstrual-related TSS learn that they have a 30 percent chance of contracting the illness again. Thus, they experience uncertainty and stress each month when menstruation occurs. Reporter Kathy Hoerstein Quirk and TSS survivor Lisa describe the emotional toll the threat of recurrence took on Lisa: "When she went home, she worried about her next period because [Dr.] Mehbod had told her the disease could possibly recur then. 'I'm still kind of paranoid about it' Lisa adds, 'now, five months later.'"[47]

Therefore, in an effort to meet this challenge, TSS survivors take a number of steps to diminish the threat of a recurrence. One key step is avoiding the use of barrier contraceptive devices such as diaphragms, cervical caps, contraceptive sponges, and intrauterine devices (IUDs), all of which can encourage the growth of *S. aureus* in susceptible individuals. Using sanitary pads rather than tampons during menstruation is also vital for women who have had menstrual-related TSS. "I certainly do not use tampons any more and caution all my friends against using them," Erin explains. "Even though TSS is rare, it's so devastating that it's not worth the risk. TSS certainly changed my life. It forced me to take a good hard look at myself, my life, my choices. I've made a lot of changes. Life is too short and you never know."[48]

Preventive Measures for Everyone

Although today cases of TSS are extremely rare, they do occur. "There's not lots and lots and lots of cases, but it's still out there,"[49] explains TSS expert, University of Minnesota, Minneapolis professor Patrick Schlievert. Therefore, taking simple preventive measures can save people's lives.

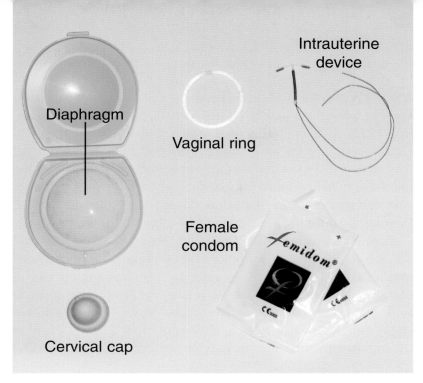

Barrier contraceptive devices like these can promote the growth of *Staphylococcus aureus*.

One important step is keeping all skin wounds, no matter how small, clean. This involves disinfecting wounds as soon as possible and covering any open sores that might come in contact with dirt or germs.

Changing bandages frequently, rather than keeping them on for several days, is also important. Since *S. aureus* carried on unwashed hands can cause an infection at the site of a microabrasion, it is essential that individuals wash their hands both before and after handling bandages. Similarly, reopening of wounds can produce portals of entry for *S. aureus*. Therefore, refraining from scratching or picking at itchy wounds and sores is another way to reduce infection. Monitoring wounds for signs of infection is also imperative. If a wound becomes red, warm, or swollen, seeing a doctor right away can help prevent TSS from developing.

For tampon users, using a tampon with the lowest degree of absorbency suitable to the user's flow is essential. A woman's menstrual flow changes from day to day, and matching tampon absorbency to flow level will decrease the risk of a tampon absorbing normal vaginal fluids. As a result, the vaginal walls are less likely to become dry and vulnerable to microabrasions. Health care experts at Playtex, a tampon manufacturer, give this advice: "Always use the lowest absorbency to meet your needs. This helps reduce any chance of TSS. Because your period changes daily, on light-flow days, you might want to use Regular absorbency. On heavy days—go with Super."[50]

Plastic applicators that help users insert tampons can also scratch vaginal walls. Tampons with cardboard applicators are available, however, and it is safer to insert a tampon with a cardboard applicator than with a finger: Like plastic applicators, fingernails can abrade the vaginal walls. In addition, because individuals can carry *S. aureus* on their fingers, washing the hands with soap and warm water before and after inserting

According to experts, sanitary napkins (left and center) are less likely to cause toxic shock syndrome than tampons (lower right).

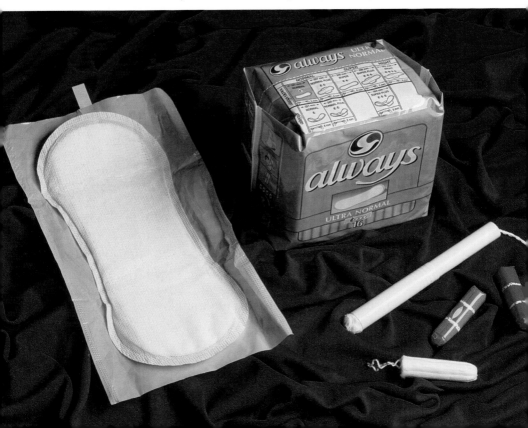

a tampon is essential. For the same reason, hand washing is crucial before and after inserting or removing diaphragms and contraceptive sponges.

Since the longer any device is left in place, the more chance for bacterial growth, removing barrier contraceptives and changing tampons often is vital. Experts say diaphragms or contraceptive sponges should not be left inside a woman's vagina for more than eighteen to twenty-four hours. According to health care professionals, tampons should not be worn for more than eight hours. Indeed, changing them every four to six hours is best. Tanis, a young woman who follows these measures, explains:

> I don't keep tampons in for more than 1 to 2 hours usually. . . . I've talked to some girls who wear tampons all the time, even when they go to bed. I've told them time and time again to never do that because the risk of TSS is definitely higher when you use them . . . overnight. They seem to think that it's not that big a deal and that it's so rare it wouldn't happen to them.[51]

But, despite the condition's rarity, wearing a tampon overnight is risky. Wearing a pad instead keeps bacterial colonies from growing while a woman is asleep. Indeed, avoiding continual use of tampons limits bacterial contact with the body, which is why it is wise to alternate tampons with pads whenever it is possible. In explaining how young women can best protect themselves, TSS expert Dr. James K. Todd gives this advice: "Adolescent girls should be encouraged to use the lowest absorbency tampon that will still control their flow, to change tampons frequently (every four to six hours) and to use pads instead of tampons at night."[52]

It is clear that although TSS is a rare condition, when it does strike it takes a toll on its victims. Recovering patients face a number of challenges, not least of which is the threat of recurrence. By taking steps to reduce the possibility of the condition recurring, survivors can help protect themselves from further damage. Similar steps help others from developing the illness.

CHAPTER FIVE

Protecting the Public Now and in the Future

Scientists are investigating *Staphylococcus aureus* and its effect on the immune system. Through these studies, they hope to develop new methods of disabling the pathogen, which is responsible for many illnesses in addition to TSS. At the same time, public health agencies and tampon manufacturers have taken steps to make tampon use safer and are providing the public with information about TSS. These efforts should reduce the number of TSS cases and the threat the condition poses.

Protecting the Public

After the TSS outbreak of the 1980s, the FDA instituted a number of safety measures to reduce opportunities for new cases of menstrual-related TSS to develop. One of the most important steps was classifying tampons as a medical device. Previously unregulated, tampons must now undergo meticulous safety testing before being marketed to the public. As a result, a manufacturer considering any changes in the design or composition of a tampon must demonstrate that the new tampon does not encourage bacterial growth or increase the risk of ulceration of the vaginal walls. Because such testing is ongoing, the risk that women will be exposed to a new product that enhances the growth of *S. aureus* is minimized. Colin Pollard, chief of the FDA's obstetrics and gynecology device branch, explains: "We ensure tampon design and materials are safe through a solid, scientifically valid premarket review process. . . . All tampon manufacturers, including those introducing new materials, report to the FDA on absorbency, as well as on the safety of the components of a tampon."[53]

The FDA also created a standard of tampon absorbency. Before there was a standard, one tampon manufacturer's "regular absorbency" product might have been the same as another's "super absorbent." Hence, consumers seeking to protect themselves by using a less absorbent product needed more information than was available on tampon packages. To assist consumers, the FDA now requires manufacturers to perform a standardized test to measure the grams of fluid that a tampon

Tampons are now carefully regulated so that consumers can feel more confident about using them.

absorbs and limits tampon absorbency levels to no more than 0.63 ounces (18g), a level lower than super-absorbent tampons popular in the 1980s. Tampon absorbency labeling has also been standardized into five categories. The classification rating and what level the product fits into must be clearly displayed on the outside of the tampon package with a label that advises consumers to use the lowest absorbency possible to control their flow.

Educating the Public

Most experts agree that to prevent new TSS cases from developing, the public must be educated about the condition and how to prevent it. Therefore, the FDA requires that every package of tampons contain an educational insert describing the link between tampons and TSS and providing information about TSS risk factors, the warning signs of TSS, and what to do if TSS symptoms develop.

This information not only increases the individual tampon user's awareness of TSS, but tells women how to keep an attack of TSS from becoming life threatening. Cindy, a former bridal consultant, recalls that one of her clients had TSS as a teenager.

> Three days into her period she came down with a fever, a rash, and diarrhea. She went to the doctor. He had never seen a case of TSS before and didn't know what was wrong with her. But she'd read the information inside the box of tampons. She thought that the symptoms it described sounded like hers. She asked the doctor if it might be TSS. He did a swab and sent it to the lab. Sure enough, it came back TSS. She swears that reading that information saved her life.[54]

Studying *Staphylococcus aureus*

Scientists throughout the world are hoping to protect the public by investigating *Staphylococcus aureus*. Since the more that is known about a pathogen the easier it is to combat, scientists hope to learn enough about *S. aureus* to neutralize its harmful effects. This would make new cases of TSS, whether menstrual or nonmenstrual, no more dangerous than a case of the flu.

One group of scientists at the University of Chicago is investigating the sequence of events through which *S. aureus* acquires iron. All bacteria need iron to survive and reproduce,

The Robin Danielson Act

The Robin Danielson Act is a proposed law named for a woman who died of toxic shock syndrome. The bill would direct the National Institutes of Health to conduct extensive studies on whether materials used in tampons present any health risk to women. These studies would be in addition to the tests now required by law and would help determine whether such additives have any link to cancer or TSS.

The bill's sponsor, Congresswoman Carolyn B. Maloney, introduced the legislation to help American women make educated consumer decisions about tampons.

"This bill is important," she says, "because of the sheer number of women who use these products. Tampons are used by approximately 73 million American women—that's 53% of American women and almost a third of the total population."

Reporting cases of toxic shock syndrome to the Centers for Disease Control and Prevention (CDC) is currently voluntary, which means that no one knows the number of TSS cases and deaths. Underreporting is likely. The Robin Danielson Act would oblige the CDC to collect, report on, and track such data, thus raising awareness among women and their physicians of the continued risk for contracting the disease.

Quoted in Congresswoman Carolyn B. Maloney (D-NY), "Summary of Tampon Safety Legislation." www.house.gov/maloney/issues/tamponsum.html.

Scientists around the world, like this researcher in Kenya, are working to develop therapies to combat *Staphylococcus aureus.*

and *S. aureus* obtains its iron mainly by secreting hemolysin and other chemicals that break down red blood cells. If scientists can identify the steps in the pathway that enables this to happen, then they can begin to develop medications to block particular steps in the iron-gathering process. Stopping the growth and spread of *S. aureus* before toxins are released is one goal; another is to produce a medication that can be administered once infection has taken hold. Since new strains of antibiotic-resistant *S. aureus* continue to arise, making treating TSS more and more difficult, the need for such medication is plain.

Blocking the Toxin

In 2003, scientists studying *S. aureus* in a laboratory identified six different proteins, each with a particular function, which the bacteria produces in order to acquire iron. They also identified the sequence in which this happens. Members of the new protein group are known as iron-regulated surface determinants, or Isd proteins.

Preventing Antibiotic Resistance

Antibiotic use promotes resistance to antibiotics. To prevent *S. aureus* from developing resistance to even more medications, thus making treatment of TSS more challenging, health officials have instituted a campaign to reduce the demand for and the overprescription of antibiotics. According to the Centers for Disease Control and Prevention (CDC) "Smart use of antibiotics is the key to controlling the spread of resistance."

As part of this campaign, the CDC created a medical school curriculum to teach future doctors about the appropriate use of antibiotics and to develop practical decision-making skills about antibiotic use in future physicians.

Another part of the effort involves a national media campaign aimed at increasing the public's knowledge of antibiotic resistance. The target audience is parents of young children, who often ask pediatricians to administer antibiotics to their children when such treatment is inappropriate. Richard Besser, the director of the CDC's national campaign, explains: "The biggest problem is inappropriate prescribing of antibiotics. Tens of millions of antibiotics are prescribed in doctor's offices for viral infections, which are not treatable with antibiotics. . . . The best way to combat this practice is to educate the physicians and the public to decrease both demand and over prescribing."

Quoted in CDC, "Antibiotic Resistance." www.cdc.gov/drugresistance/community.

Isd proteins operate like a production line: After one protein breaks open red blood cells, other proteins grab hemoglobin from the red cells, extract the iron, and pass it on to still other proteins that carry the iron back to the bacteria. The director of the study, Olaf Schneewind, explains: "It's a beautiful system, a complete and very elegant pathway."[55]

Using this discovery as a springboard, the scientists are currently working on developing medications to derail this chain of events. Blocking any one of the Isd proteins from doing its job, for example, would deprive the bacteria of iron. Since there are six different proteins, this means that the scientists can develop different medications, each aimed at a particular protein. The need for a variety of drugs is especially apparent when dealing with *S. aureus*, which is known for quickly developing resistance to medication. Eric Skaar, coauthor of the study, continues, "Our findings could be used to develop drugs that would disrupt Staphylococcal iron uptake systems, multiple new drug targets."[56]

Blocking Cytokines

Japanese scientists are taking another tactic. They are investigating the effect on the abnormal activation of cytokines by the TSST-1 superantigen of a Chinese herbal substance with anti-inflammatory properties. The scientists theorized that the extract, anisodamine, can inhibit the production of inflammation-stimulating cytokines activated by TSST-1 and, therefore, be useful in treating TSS.

In 2004, scientists at Niigata University and Tokyo Women's Medical University School of Medicine tested their theory on white blood cells taken from donated human blood samples provided by healthy donors. The cells were treated with TSST-1 and divided into three groups. The first group was redivided and treated with increasing doses of anisodamine ranging from 10 milliliters to 40 milliliters, while the second group was treated in the same manner with a proven anti-inflammatory drug. The third group served as a control. After forty-eight hours, the cytokine levels in all three groups were measured and compared.

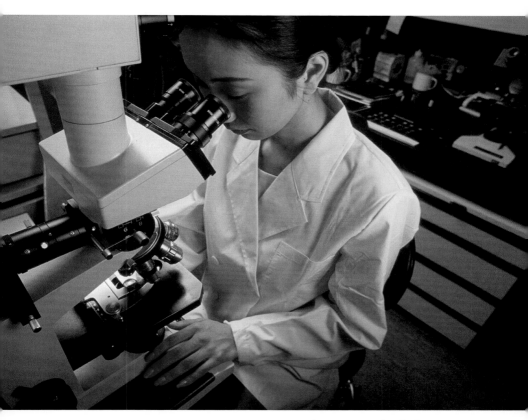

Japanese scientists are experimenting with a Chinese herb that may minimize the immune system's production of cytokine, which causes symptoms of toxic shock syndrome.

The scientists found that the cells treated with anisodamine had the lowest cytokine levels and that the levels decreased as the dosage increased. The cytokine levels reported for the group treated with standard anti-inflammatory medication were significantly higher—approximately 750 at 10 milliliter doses, 600 at 20 milliliter doses, and 500 at 40 milliliter doses. Cytokine levels in the anisodamine group measured 400 at 10 milliliter doses, 100 at 20 milliliter doses, and less than 5 at 40 milliliter doses. As a result, the scientists surmised that anisodamine not only inhibits cytokine production but is more effective than at least one traditional anti-inflammatory drug.

Based on these results, the scientists tested sixty laboratory mice to measure the effect of anisodamine on cytokine levels and survival rates. The mice were divided into three groups. Two groups were injected with TSST-1, while the control group was injected with a harmless saline solution. Ten minutes later, one group that had received the superantigen was injected with anisodamine at a dose equivalent to 50 milligrams per pound of their body weight, while the second group was untreated. For the next five days, the survival rate of each group was monitored, and cytokine levels were measured via blood samples.

As in the first study, the results were promising. Cytokine levels in the group treated with anisodamine were not only significantly lower than those of the untreated group, they were almost equivalent to those in the control group. Survival rates were also encouraging. The scientists reported 100 percent survival rate in the control group and the anisodamine-treated group, but only 40 percent in the untreated group. In a report in the scientific journal *Clinical and Diagnostic Laboratory Immunology*, the researchers explain: "We demonstrated that the levels of cytokines induced by TSST-1 in serum were significantly reduced by anisodamine and that anisodamine indeed protected the mice against the lethal effect of TSST-1. . . . The Chinese medicine anisodamine . . . may be a potential drug for the treatment of TSST-1-mediated diseases."[57]

Because to be most effective anisodamine doses must be quite high, the Japanese scientists are continuing with animal experiments. Once they are confident that the needed dosage can be delivered safely, human tests will begin. Scientists hope that anisodamine intravenous therapy will eventually be used to stop, or greatly reduce, the damaging effects of TSST-1 on infected individuals.

Blocking T-Cell Activation

Israeli scientists at the Hebrew University-Hadassah Medical School in Jerusalem are also working to reduce the autoimmune response to superantigens. But instead of focusing solely on cytokine production, which occurs after superantigens have activated T cells, they are trying to block the activation of T cells entirely. This involves using protein molecules known as peptide antagonists that block the ability of TSST-1 and enterotoxins SEA and SEB to activate T cells.

In 2001, the scientists created P-12 and P-14, two synthetic peptides made up of twelve and fourteen amino acids, respectively, which bind to a T cell at the same receptor site used by superantigens. The scientists theorized that if the superantigens were prevented from binding to the T cells because the peptide antagonists were already there, T cells could not be activated, and thus the inflammatory cascade could not begin.

At Hebrew University in Jerusalem, pictured here, Israeli scientists are working on ways to block the activation of T cells, which are part of the immune system's response to superantigens.

The scientists first tested their theory on human white blood cells. Some of the cells were injected with P-12 shortly before being exposed to the superantigen SEB, while the others, as a control group, were not. Then, T-cell activation in the form of cytokine production was measured in both groups. When the results were compared, the untreated group showed high T-cell activation, whereas T-cell activation and the release of cytokines had been almost completely blocked in the white blood cells treated with P-12.

Using lab mice, Israeli scientists successfully tested their experimental treatment to block the activation of T cells.

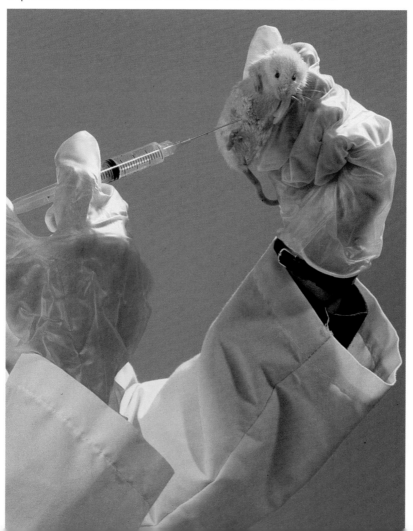

The ability of P-12 to block the inflammatory cascade in human cells in a test tube led the scientists to examine whether it or P-14 would have a similar effect on mice. This experiment involved three groups of mice, the first two of which were injected with P-14. One of these groups acted as the control. Thirty minutes later, the noncontrol group and a third group were exposed to lethal doses of SEB. Within twenty hours, 90 percent of the mice that were not treated with P-14 died. Conversely, 90 percent of the group that was inoculated with P-14 and exposed to SEB survived. In addition, all of the subjects in the control group—the mice that had been treated with P-14 but not exposed to the superantigen—survived and exhibited no ill effects from inoculation with the peptide antagonist.

Survivors in the group exposed to SEB and P-14 were monitored for two weeks and showed no sign of inflammation or illness during this time. The scientists reproduced this experiment fifteen times with similar results. They also reported similar results with P-12.

Another Theory

Since the results of these experiments seemed to be so conclusive, the scientists wondered whether P-14 would have any protective effect when not administered until after exposure to SEB. To test this theory, they designed another controlled experiment, this one involving five groups of mice, two of which were control groups. In one portion of the experiment, mice in each of the three non-control groups were exposed to SEB and treated with P-14 at intervals of three, five, and seven hours afterward, respectively. Survival rates were compared over a twenty-four-hour period. Many of these mice survived, although a progressively decreasing protection rate was recorded: 70 percent at three hours, 60 percent at five hours, and 50 percent at seven hours. The experiment was repeated using P-12 in lieu of P-14, with similar results. After the demonstration that the peptide antagonists can protect and rescue mammalian subjects from the effects of a superantigen, the Israeli investigators began human clinical trials. They are hopeful that in the future, P-12 and P-14 will be available for widespread use in treating TSS. Study director Raymond Kaempfer explains: "Because the patented protein molecule is simple and relatively cheap to produce, and has shown no harmful side effects, such a drug could be given safely to emergency-room patients showing the first signs of toxic shock."[58]

A Possible Vaccine

Having seen that peptide antagonists have a short-term protective effect against toxic shock superantigen SEB, the Israeli scientists wanted to know if the proteins were also effective against superantigens SEA and TSST-1. If such an effect in fact existed and was maintained over time, P-12 or P-14 could be used as a vaccine against TSS. To study this question, the scientists exposed ten of the surviving mice that had been previously treated with P-14 to SEA. Seven of these ten mice survived. Two weeks later, the seven survivors were reexposed to SEB, and all the mice survived. Two weeks thereafter, the mice were exposed to TSST-1, with only one fatality. In comparison, all of the mice in all three control groups had died after exposure to SEB. The scientists concluded:

> The anatagonist protects mice from killing by a range of staphylococcal . . . superantigens. . . . What is more, it rescues mice from undergoing toxic shock. The protected animals rapidly develop a broad-spectrum protective immunity against further lethal toxin challenges from the same superantigen and even with superantigen toxins that they have not encountered before.[59]

The results indicate that the immune system of individuals inoculated with a vaccine made up of peptide antagonists might be able to disable the superantigens. Currently, Israeli scientists, with the support of the U.S. National Institutes of Health, are working on developing such a vaccine. Scientists are hopeful that by rendering *S. aureus* infections relatively harmless, such a vaccine will safeguard the public from the effect of the superantigens.

Another Approach

American scientists are also busy developing a vaccine. This ongoing project began in 1998 and involves scientists at Nabi Biopharmaceuticals of Boca Raton, Florida, in conjunction with scientists at a number of universities and hospitals throughout the United States. Rather than targeting the super-antigens, the vaccine these scientists are working on targets *S. aureus* itself. Specifically, it aims to increase the bacteria's vulnerability to antibodies by removing the protection provided by polysaccharides, the sugar molecules that form a defensive outer covering around *S. aureus.*

The researchers know that antibodies specific to polysaccharides are capable of breaking through the polysaccharide capsule that surrounds *S. aureus* and engulfing the bacteria. However, because the immune system does not recognize the polysaccharides *S. aureus* secretes as a threat, it does not produce the antibodies against the bacteria. If, the researchers theorize, they can create a polysaccharide-based substance that the immune system recognizes as a foreign substance, this would trigger the release of the appropriate antibodies. The antibodies would then become part of the immune system's arsenal. As a result, subsequent exposure to *S. aureus* would trigger the release of these protective antibodies and the destruction of the bacteria.

If such a vaccine could be developed, it could be administered to people most at risk of developing TSS. These include individuals with weakened immune systems, people in danger of going into shock, people undergoing kidney dialysis, and people who have had TSS in the past. It could also be given to individuals before they undergo nasal and other surgeries.

With this in mind, the scientists developed a substance known as StaphVax. This vaccine consists of polysaccharides derived from *S. aureus* combined with a bacterial toxin that has been rendered harmless by means of genetic engineering.

Early StaphVax tests on mice yielded such encouraging results that human trials began in 2000. These tests involved controlled testing on U.S. volunteers at risk of developing TSS or

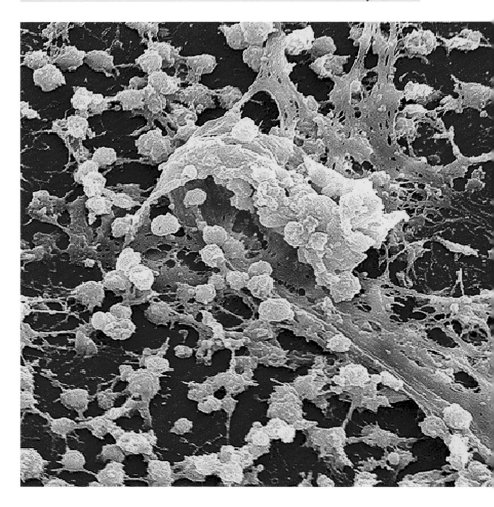

other staph infections. In these tests, half of the subjects were inoculated with StaphVax, while the other half received a placebo (a substance with no medicinal value, such as a sugar solution). Then the subjects' antibody levels were monitored over a fifty-four-week period, as were *S. aureus* infection rates.

Among the subjects receiving the vaccine, *S. aureus* antibody levels increased dramatically for two weeks, then leveled out and disappeared after forty weeks. During this time period, the vaccinated group exhibited 69 percent fewer *S. aureus* infections as compared to the placebo group.

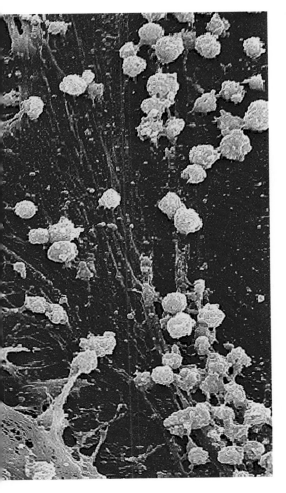

The bacterium *Staphylococcus aureus*, a colony is pictured here, is the focus of scientists who are working to defeat toxic shock syndrome.

A Final Hurdle, a Promising Future

Results thus far show that the vaccine offers protection over the short term only. Researchers theorize that administering repeated doses of the vaccine should solve this problem. As of November 2005, the results had not yet been determined, but scientists are hopeful. "The fact that the vaccine prevents infection rather than stopping it after it starts, offers new avenues of prophylaxis [preventive treatment] in many high-risk situations,"[60] explains Henry Shinefield, who is directing one of the trials at Kaiser Permanente Vaccine Study Center in Oakland, California.

It is clear that scientists are working hard to minimize the threat TSS poses. New treatments and possible vaccines offer innovative methods to control *S. aureus* and the superantigens. Ongoing safety measures, which protect and educate the public, are also having a positive impact. It is not surprising, then, that TSS cases are rare. In fact, with all the work being done, it is possible that the illness will become only a memory in the future.

Notes

Introduction: Knowledge Is Crucial

1. Quoted in Kathy Hoersten Quirk, "Toxic Shock Syndrome" Quirk Ink. www.quirkink.com/quirkink/toxic.htm.
2. Dixie Farley, "On the Teen Scene: TSS: Reducing the Risk," U.S. Food and Drug Administration. www.fda.gov/bbs/topics/consumer/con00116.html.
3. Quoted in Quirk, "Toxic Shock Syndrome."
4. Quoted in Julie Severns Lyons, "A New Generation Faces Toxic Shock Syndrome," *Seattle Times*, January 26, 2005. http://seattletimes.nwsource.com/html/health/2002160362 _healthtoxicshock26.html.
5. Bea, interview with the author, August 19, 2005, Las Cruces, NM.

Chapter 1: A Mysterious Illness

6. Quoted in Laurie Garrett, *The Coming Plague.* New York: Penguin, 1994, p. 396.
7. Quoted in Tom Riley, *The Price of a Life.* Bethesda, MD: Adler & Adler, 1986, p. 42.
8. Riley, *The Price of a Life*, p. 8.
9. Quoted in Riley, *The Price of a Life*, p. 157.
10. Riley, *The Price of a Life*, p. 48.
11. Quoted in Garrett, *The Coming Plague*, p. 363.
12. Dr. Robert V. Hoffman, interview with the author, October 4, 2005, Las Cruces, NM.
13. Quoted in Riley, *The Price of a Life*, p. 36.
14. Quoted in Nancy Friedman, "Everything They Didn't Tell You About Tampons," *New West*, October 1980, pp. 33–42.
15. Hoffman, interview.

Chapter 2:
Overactivating the Immune System

16. Hoffman, interview.
17. Dr. John E. Gustafson, interview with the author, October 4, 2005, Las Cruces, NM.
18. Alice Kilvert Tampon Alert, "Case Studies." www.tampon alert.org.uk/akta/casestud.htm.
19. Gustafson, interview.
20. Quoted in Alice Kilvert Tampon Alert, "What's New." www.tamponalert.org.uk/akta/whatsnew.htm.
21. Quoted in Michelle Ribeiro and Patti Greco, "I Almost Died of Toxic Shock Syndrome," *Cosmo Girl*, December 2004/January 2005, p. 96.
22. Gustafson, interview.
23. Quoted in Ribeiro and Greco, "I Almost Died of Toxic Shock Syndrome," p. 96.
24. Riley, *The Price of a Life*, p. 109.
25. Rose, interview with the author, October 4, 2005, Las Cruces, NM.
26. Quoted in Ribeiro and Greco, "I Almost Died of Toxic Shock Syndrome," p. 96.
27. Abigail Salyers and Dixie D. Whitt, *Bacterial Pathogenesis, A Molecular Approach*. Washington, DC: American Society of Microbiology, 2001, p. 56.
28. Quoted in Quirk, "Toxic Shock Syndrome."

Chapter 3: A Medical Emergency

29. Farley, "On the Teen Scene: TSS: Reducing the Risk."
30. Alice Kilvert Tampon Alert, "Case Studies."
31. Quoted in Rick Alan, "TSS: Tampon and More," Mountain View Regional Medical Center. www.mountainviewregional.com/healthcontent.asp?form=1&page=/transfer/search/processSearchRequest&featureid=HGConsumerContent&siteid=.
32. Quoted in Riley, *The Price of a Life*, p. 10.
33. Ferhat Erisir, "Toxic Shock Syndrome Following Endoscopic Surgery," *Turkish Archives of Otolaryngology*, 2001, p. 306.

34. Gustafson, interview.
35. Quoted in Alice Kilvert Tampon Alert, "Case Studies."
36. Quoted in Quirk, "Toxic Shock Syndrome."

Chapter 4: Recovery and Prevention

37. Quoted in Alice Kilvert Tampon Alert, "What's New."
38. Crossroads: Real People, "Lisa Clark (Mengarelli)," www.crossroader.org/people/lisa.html.
39. Crossroads: Real People, "Lisa Clark (Mengarelli)."
40. Crossroads: Real People, "Lisa Clark (Mengarelli)."
41. Quoted in Alice Kilvert Tampon Alert, "What's New."
42. Robin, interview with the author, September 2, 2005, Radium Springs, NM.
43. Quoted in Quirk, "Toxic Shock Syndrome."
44. Crossroads: Real People, "Lisa Clark (Mengarelli)."
45. Willi Nolan, "Toxic Shock Is a Nightmare: The Story of a Survivor," Terra Femme Tampons, www.web.net/terra femme/cashnightmare.htm.
46. Toxic Shock Syndrome Information Service of Australia, "Frequently Asked Questions about TSS." www.toxic shock.org.au/faqs/main.asp.
47. Quirk, "Toxic Shock Syndrome."
48. Quoted in Alice Kilvert Tampon Alert, "What's New."
49. Quoted in Lyons, "A New Generation Faces Toxic Shock Syndrome."
50. Playtex Tampons, "Menstrual Myths." www.playtex tampons.com/body/menstruation_myths.html.
51. Quoted in Alice Kilvert Tampon Alert, "What's New."
52. James K. Todd, "Toxic Shock Syndrome," The Children's Hospital. www.pediatricweb.com/tchDenver/article.asp? ArticleID=857&ArticleType=9.

Chapter 5: Protecting the Public Now and in the Future

53. Quoted in Michelle Meadows, "Tampon Safety: TSS Now Rare, but Women Still Should Take Care," *FDA Consumer Magazine*, March/April 2000, p. 20.
54. Cindy, interview with the author, September 14, 2005, Las Cruces, NM.

55. Quoted in University of Chicago Hospitals, "Discovery of Iron-Acquisition Pathway Suggests New Treatment for Drug-Resistant Staph. Infections," February 6, 2003. www.uchospitals.edu/news/2003/20030206-staph-get-iron.html.

56. Quoted in University of Chicago Hospitals, "Discovery of Iron-Acquisition Pathway Suggests New Treatment for Drug-Resistant Staph. Infections."

57. Saori Nakagawa, Koji Kushiya, Ikue Taneike, Ken'ichi Imanishi, Takehiko Uchiyama, and Tatsuo Yamamoto, "Specific Inhibitory Action of Anisodamine Against a Staphylococcal Superantigen Toxin, Toxic Shock Syndrome Toxin 1 (TSST-1), Leading to Down-Regulation of Cytokine Production and Blocking of TSST-1 Toxicity in Mice," Clinical and Diagnostic Laboratory Immunology, March 2005. http://cdli.asm.org/cgi/content/abstract/12/3/399.

58. Quoted in Judy Siegel-Itzkovich, Israel Ministry of Foreign Affairs, "Shock Treatment," Israel Magazine-on-Web, June 2000. www.israel-mfa.gov.il/MFA/Israel%20beyond%20the%20conflict/Shock%20Treat . . .

59. Quoted in Kaempfer Lab, "Research Projects—Superantigen Antagonist Protects Against Lethal Shock and Defines a New Domain for T-Cell Activation." http://molvirology.huji.ac.il/research6.htm.

60. Quoted in Donna Hoel, "How Close Is a Staph Vaccine?" Postgraduate Medicine Online, October 2001. www.postgraduatemed.com/issues/2001/10_01/hoel.htm.

Glossary

abscess: A collection of pus caused by an infection in the skin.

antibiotic resistance: The ability of a strain of bacteria to flourish when exposed to drugs to which they were once susceptible.

antibody: A naturally occurring protein produced by the immune system to defend the body from foreign substances.

antigen: A substance that activates the production of an antibody when it enters the body.

capillary: A small blood vessel.

cytokines: Proteins that initiate an inflammatory response when released by white blood cells called T cells.

emergent disease: A disease that was once rare but has suddenly become more common and threatens to increase in the future.

enterotoxin A, B, and C (SEA, SEB, SEC): Three distinct superantigens produced by *Staphylococcus aureus*.

epidemiologist: A medical expert who investigates the transmission and control of epidemic diseases.

immunoglobin: Pooled blood plasma.

inflammation: The body's response to infection. It is characterized by heat, redness, and swelling, and often elicits fever, diarrhea, vomiting, and vasodilation.

iron-regulated surface determinants (Isd proteins): Proteins bacteria release in order to gather iron.

macrophage: A large cell that removes waste material and foreign objects from the bloodstream.

mucous membrane: The lining of body passages that are in contact in some way with the exterior of the body or the environment.

pathogen: A living substance that causes disease, such as a virus or bacteria.

plasma: The liquid part of the blood that carries antibodies.

red blood cells: Iron-rich blood cells that carry oxygen throughout the body.

shock: A medical emergency characterized by the collapse of the circulatory system.

Staphylococcus aureus (S. aureus): A toxin-producing bacteria that is known to cause toxic shock syndrome.

superantigen: Bacterial toxins that stimulate an exaggerated immune response.

T cells: White blood cells that act like the controls of the immune response.

toxins: Poisons or proteins that act as poisons in the body.

TSST-1: A superantigen produced by *Staphylococcus aureus.*

vasodilation: A process in which blood vessels widen or dilate in order to allow more blood to pass through.

white blood cells: Cells whose job it is to attack and destroy foreign substances in the bloodstream.

Organizations to Contact

Alice Kilvert Tampon Alert

16 Blinco Rd. Urmston, Manchester, England M419NF
Phone: 0161-748-3123
tamponalert@ntl.world.com
www.tamponalert.org.uk

This British organization was formed by the family and friends of Alice Kilvert, who died of toxic shock syndrome at age fifteen. The organization offers information about toxic shock syndrome, answers questions, and provides support.

U.S. Centers for Disease Control and Prevention

1600 Clifton Rd. NE, Atlanta, GA 30333
(800) 311-3435
www.cdc.gov

This Web site offers information about disease outbreaks, antibiotic-resistant *S. aureus*, and toxic shock syndrome.

Congresswoman Carolyn B. Maloney (D-NY)

1651 Third Ave., Suite 311, New York, NY 10128-3679
(212) 860-0606
Fax: (212) 860-0704
www.house.gov/maloney/index.html

This Web site provides information about the Robin Danielson Act. The congresswoman can be e-mailed directly from her Web site.

National Women's Health Network

514 Tenth St. NW, Suite 400, Washington, D.C. 20004

(202) 628-7814
nwhn@nwhn.org
www.womenshealthnetwork.org

This nonprofit health organization provides information on women's health issues, including TSS.

Toxic Shock Syndrome Information Service
P.O. Box 6463, North Sydney, Australia, NSW 2060
www.toxicshock.org

This Australian organization provides free information about toxic shock syndrome. The organization can be e-mailed directly from its Web site.

U.S. Food and Drug Administration
5600 Fisher La., Rockville, MD 20857
webmail@oc.fda.gov
www.fda.gov

This Web site provides information about toxic shock syndrome, *S. aureus*, and antibiotic resistance.

For Further Reading

Books

Boston Women's Health Book Collective, *Our Bodies, Ourselves*. New York: Touchstone, 2005. A simple reference book that discusses all types of health issues affecting women, including TSS.

James N. Parker and Philip M. Parker, *The Official Patient's Sourcebook on Toxic Shock Syndrome*. San Diego: Icon Group International, 2002. This book provides a wide range of references to help people research TSS.

Brian Shmaefsky, *Toxic Shock Syndrome*. Philadelphia: Chelsea House, 2004. A young adult book that looks at TSS as an emerging disease as well as discusses *S. aureus*.

Periodicals

Michelle Meadows, "Tampon Safety: TSS Now Rare, but Women Still Should Take Care," *FDA Consumer Magazine*, March/April 2000. Gives information about TSS and preventive measures.

Michelle Ribeiro and Patti Greco, "I Almost Died of Toxic Shock Syndrome," *Cosmo Girl*, December 2004/January 2005. A young woman talks about her experience with TSS.

Internet Sources

BBC, "Real Life Stories." www.bbc.co.uk/teens/girls/sexlove andlife/reallifestories/tss.shtml. Sarah, a TSS survivor, tells her story.

Nemours Foundation, "Toxic Shock Syndrome." www.kids health.org/teen/sexual_health/girls/tss.html. An informative article about menstrual TSS with a look at symptoms and preventive measures.

ObGyn Center On-line, "Toxic Shock Syndrome." http://obgyn. healthcentersonline.com/menstruation/toxicshocksyn drome.cfm. Doctors specializing in women's health issues provide information about TSS, including its diagnosis, treatment, and prevention.

Web Sites

Playtex (www.playtextampons.com). This tampon manufac- turer offers information about menstruation, tampon use, and TSS prevention.

Tampax (www.tampax.com). This tampon manufacturer of- fers information about menstruation, tampon use, and TSS prevention. It has a special section for teens.

Toxic Shock Syndrome Information Service (www.toxic shock.com). This British organization provides online infor- mation about TSS, including a downloadable pamphlet.

Index

Picture Credits

About the Author

Barbara Sheen has been an author and educator for more than thirty years. Her work has been published in the United States and Europe. She lives in New Mexico with her family. In her spare time, she likes to swim, garden, walk, cook, and read.